D

Writing in the Disciplines

Advice and Models

*Supplement to Accompany
Diana Hacker's*

A Writer's Reference

Sixth Edition

Tom Jehn
Harvard University

Jane Rosenzweig
Harvard University

Writing in the Disciplines Specialist

Terry Myers Zawacki
George Mason University

BEDFORD / ST. MARTIN'S   Boston ◆ New York

Discipline Specialists

For their assistance and advice as discipline specialists, we thank the following: Jules Benjamin, Ithaca College (history); Dorinda J. Carter, Michigan State University (education); Jennifer DeForest, University of Virginia (education); Susan Durham, George Mason University (nursing); Victoria McMillan, Colgate University (biology); James Morris, Harvard University (biology); Kirsten Olson, Wheaton College (education); Sherry Robertson, Arizona State University (business); and Beth Schneider, George Mason University (business).

Manufactured in the United States of America.

2   1   0   9   8   7
f   e   d   c   b   a

For information, write: Bedford/St. Martin's, 75 Arlington Street, Boston, MA 02116   (617-399-4000)

ISBN-10: 0-312-45264-0
ISBN-13: 978-0-312-45264-3

Acknowledgments

Jules Benjamin, "Wage Slavery or True Independence? Women Workers in the Lowell, Massachusetts, Textile Mills, 1820–1850," excerpt from *A Student's Guide to History,* Ninth Edition. Copyright © 2004 by Bedford/St. Martin's. Reprinted with permission. "1845 Map of Lowell." Reprinted by permission of the Lowell Historical Society. "Regulations for the Boarding Houses of the Middlesex Company." Reprinted by permission of the American Textile History Museum, Lowell, MA.

Valerie Charat, "Always Out of Their Seats (and Fighting): Why Are Boys Diagnosed with ADHD More Often Than Girls?" (December 15, 2006). Reprinted with permission.

Onnalee L. Gibson, "A Reflection on Service Learning: Working with Eric" (April 25, 2006). Reprinted with permission.

Marin Johnson and Laura Arnold, "Distribution Pattern of Dandelion (*Taraxacum officinale*) on an Abandoned Golf Course" (September 13, 2005). Reprinted with permission.

Victoria McMillan, excerpt from *Writing Papers in the Biological Sciences,* Fourth Edition. Copyright © 2006 by Bedford/St. Martin's. Reprinted with permission.

Kelly Ratajczak, "Proposal to Add a Wellness Program" (April 21, 2006). Reprinted with permission.

Julie Riss, "Acute Lymphoblastic Leukemia and Hypertension in One Client: A Nursing Practice Paper," (May 18, 2006). Reprinted with permission.

Brian Spencer, "Positively Affecting Employee Motivation" (March 9, 2006). Reprinted with permission.

D

Writing in the Disciplines: Advice and Models

D Writing in the Disciplines

D1

Introduction: Writing in different disciplines

Succeeding in college requires performing well in different kinds of courses and on various kinds of assignments. As you probably know, you will be assigned writing in your college writing courses. It may surprise you to know, however, that other college courses require writing—courses you might not expect, like nursing and psychology. The strategies you develop in your first-year composition course will help you write well in other academic courses.

The academic community is divided into broad subject areas called *disciplines*. The disciplines are generally grouped into five major fields of study, which are further broken down into more specific subjects. The five disciplines and a few representative subjects are social sciences (psychology and sociology); natural sciences (biology and chemistry); mathematics and computer science; humanities and arts (history, literature, music); and professions and applied sciences (business, education, nursing).

Each discipline has its own set of expectations and conventions for both reading and writing. Some of the expectations and conventions—writing with a clear main idea, for instance—are common across disciplines; those are covered in *A Writer's Reference*. Other expectations and conventions are unique to each discipline. These include the following:

- purpose for writing
- questions asked by scholars and practitioners
- types of evidence used
- language and writing conventions
- citation style

When you are asked to write in a specific discipline, start by becoming familiar with the distinctive features of writing in that discipline. For example, if you are asked to write a lab report for a biology class, your purpose might be to present results of an experiment. Your evidence would be the data you collected while conducting your experiment, and you would use scientific terms in your report. You would also use the CSE (Council of Science Editors) guidelines for citation of your sources. If you are asked to write a case study for an education class, your purpose might be to analyze student-teacher interactions in a single classroom. Your evidence might be data on a combination of personal observations and interviews. You would use terms from the field in your case study and cite your sources using the guidelines of the American Psychological Association (APA).

The following sections provide guidelines for writing in six disciplines: biology, business, education, history, nursing, and psychology. Each section begins with advice about the expectations for writing in that discipline and includes a model or two of student writing. Each section closes with references to professional documents in that discipline.

D2

Writing in the biological sciences

Biologists use writing in many ways. They write reports analyzing the data they collect from their experiments as well as reviews of other scientists' research or proposed research. They write proposals to convince funding agencies to award grants for their research. If they teach, biologists also write lectures. Some biologists may communicate with a general audience by writing newspaper and magazine articles. In addition, they may lend their expertise to public-policy decision making by government officials, weighing in on, say, the issue of global warming or stem cell research.

Depending on their audience, biologists—including botanists, geneticists, and zoologists—use different tones and styles in their writing. When they present their research to colleagues, they adopt a neutral voice and avoid flowery prose. Researchers also use specialized vocabulary that other biologists readily understand. When biologists write for readers of newspapers and magazines, they may use language accessible to people who are not specialists in biology. In any case, biologists strive to communicate complex information efficiently, clearly, and carefully.

When you write in biology courses, your goal will generally be to convince readers of the validity of conclusions you draw from observations, experimental data, or your evaluations of previously published or proposed research. For most assignments, you will need to use a scientific style of writing, conveying your information to readers as succinctly and accurately as possible.

D2-a Recognize the forms of writing in the biological sciences.

When you take courses in biology, you may be asked to write any of the following:

- laboratory notebooks
- research papers
- laboratory reports
- literature reviews
- research proposals
- poster presentations

Laboratory notebooks

If your class requires you to complete laboratory exercises, you will need to carefully record your laboratory experiments in a notebook. A laboratory notebook should be detailed and accurate so that anyone who wishes to repeat your experiment can do so. The laboratory notebook also provides crucial material for any report or article you may write later about your experiment. Researchers take notebooks seriously, never removing a page or erasing entries. That practice keeps them from misrepresenting results.

Your notebook will typically have the following components:

- table of contents
- date of each experiment
- title
- purpose (the objective of the experiment)
- materials (a list of equipment, specimens, and chemicals you used in the experiment)
- procedures (the method you planned to follow as well as the alterations you made to that procedure while conducting the experiment)
- acknowledgments (those who helped you with the experiment)
- results (the data gathered from the experiment)
- data analysis (calculations based on your data)
- discussion (your assessment of whether the experiment was successful, your interpretation of your results, your accounting for any surprising results, and your conclusions about what you learned from the experiment)

Research papers and laboratory reports

When instructors refer to "research papers," they may have different assignments in mind. One assignment might ask you to present your synthesis of many sources of information about, for instance, a genetic syndrome to demonstrate your understanding of the characteristics of the disorder and other researchers' investigations of the causes of the syndrome.

Another assignment might require you to report on the results of an experiment you conducted and to interpret your results; this document is typically called a *laboratory report*. Unlike the laboratory notebook, a lab report may relate your interpretations to what others in the field have concluded from their own experiments. Biologists publish research papers and reports in journals after the papers have undergone rigorous and impartial review by other biologists, called a *peer review*, to make sure that the scientific process used by the researchers is sound.

Whether published in a journal or written for a college course, research papers and reports based on original experiments follow a standard format and include the following sections:

- abstract (a 100-to-125-word summary of your report)
- introduction (the context for your experiment, such as what has been published on the topic in the field, as well as the purpose of the experiment)
- materials and methods (details of how you conducted the experiment so that other researchers can repeat the experiment to try to reproduce your results; your description of the methodology you used so that readers can determine if your interpretations are supported by the data)
- results (a presentation of what you observed in the experiment)
- figures and tables
- discussion (your interpretation of the results as well as a comparison of your interpretation and that of other researchers in the field)
- references (a list of the sources cited in your paper)

Literature reviews

Literature reviews can have different objectives, such as comparing or contrasting approaches to a problem or examining the literature in the field to propose an alternative theory. Another purpose is to inform biologists about the latest advances in the field. In a review, you will consider the findings of a number of research papers and evaluate those papers' conclusions and perhaps suggest a direction for future research. A critical review analyzes the methods and interpretations of data from one or more journal articles. A literature review also may be an introduction to a larger piece of writing, such as a report of an empirical study. In that case, the review surveys previously published findings relevant to the question that the empirical study investigates.

A literature review assignment is an opportunity to learn about an area in the field and to see what old or new questions may benefit from research.

While the format of reviews varies with their purpose, reviews typically have an abstract, an introduction, a discussion of the research being reviewed, a conclusion, and a references section.

Research proposals

In a research proposal, the biologist poses a significant question and a hypothesis (or hypotheses) and suggests one or more experiments to test the hypothesis. The project can have specific practical applications; for example, one Arctic biologist submitted to the United States Geological Survey a proposal for an ecological monitoring program at a national park. Research proposals that seek funding for an experiment must include detailed budgets.

Whether written by scholars requesting support from an agency or by students in a course, research proposals are evaluated for how well they justify their project with a carefully conceived experiment design.

Poster presentations

At professional gatherings such as annual conventions in the field, biologists have the opportunity to present their work in the form of a poster rather than as a formal talk. Conference attendees approach presenters in an exhibit area to talk about their research, which the posters concisely summarize. A poster features a brief introduction to the presenter's research project, a description of the method, information about the experiment's subjects, the experiment's results, and the presenter's conclusions. Poster presentations also feature graphs and tables since it is important to convey information to the audience quickly and concisely as they walk through the exhibit area. An effective poster presentation will encourage the audience to ask questions and carry on an informal conversation with the presenter.

Your instructor may ask you to create a poster presentation about an experiment you or other researchers have conducted both to help you understand complex concepts and to practice your communication skills.

NOTE: Some presenters use presentation software to create a slide show that they can click through for a small audience or project on a screen for a larger group. Presenters generally include the same kinds of information in slide presentations as they do in poster presentations.

D2-b Know the questions biologists ask.

Biologists, like other scientists, ask questions about the natural world. Their questions are either *why* questions or *how* questions, such as the following:

- Why don't newborns see well?
- Why does body size of species skew to the right on a distribution curve? That is, why are there so many small animals?
- How does cellular senescence prevent cancer?
- How do island plants self-pollinate?

As they attempt to answer such questions, biologists first offer a tentative explanation, or hypothesis, for something they have observed. They perform an experiment to test their hypothesis. If the results from the experiment match the original predictions, then they consider the hypothesis supported, but not proved, since the biologist cannot account for all conditions. Other biologists will continue to formulate new hypotheses and offer new findings.

D2-c Understand the kinds of evidence biologists use.

Biologists use many kinds of evidence:

- data from site studies or site surveys
- observations of specimens with the aid of special equipment, such as a microscope
- observations and measurements made in experimental settings
- data taken from reports that other biologists have published

Data in biology, which are either quantitative (that which can be counted) or qualitative (that which can be described without numbers), can take various forms, depending on the nature of the site, the type of experiment, or the specialized field in which the research is performed. Following are some examples:

- For a study of mating choices of female swordfish, biologists might record and analyze responses from females placed in tanks with males.
- In forensic biology, researchers might interpret the data they collect from tests on criminal suspects' DNA samples.
- Plant biologists might analyze the rates of survival of native tree seedlings affected by chemicals released by invasive plant species.

Because evidence can have more than one plausible interpretation, biologists offer alternative explanations for the results obtained in experiments. For example, the authors of one article suggested that differences in the type and availability of prey could account for why Atlantic blue marlin larvae grew faster in one body of water than in another, but they also recognized that other possible causes related to differences in spawning populations.

D2-d Become familiar with writing conventions in the biological sciences.

Biologists agree on several conventions when they write:

- Scientific writing often uses the passive voice to describe how a researcher has performed an experiment (*Blue marlin larvae were collected*). The passive voice can be useful for drawing attention to the action itself, not to who has performed the action. But biologists increasingly use the active voice whenever possible to convey information clearly and efficiently (*Researchers collected blue marlin larvae*). As the use of the active voice becomes widespread in scientific writing, the use of *I* and *we* is acceptable, even preferred, if the passive voice creates awkward-sounding sentences and adds unnecessary words.
- Direct quotation of sources is rare; instead, biologists paraphrase to demonstrate their understanding of the source material and to convey information economically.
- Biologists use the past tense to describe the materials and methods and the results of their own experiments.
- Biologists use the present tense to describe the published findings of other studies.

- Biologists often include specific scientific names for species (*Hyla cinerea* for the green treefrog, for instance).

D2-e Use the CSE system for citing sources.

Biologists typically use the style recommended by the Council of Science Editors (CSE) to format their paper, to cite sources in the text of the paper, and to list the sources at the end. The CSE describes three citation systems in *Scientific Style and Format: The CSE Manual for Authors, Editors, and Publishers*, 7th ed. (Reston: CSE, 2006). In the *name-year* system, the author's last name and the date of publication are cited in the text. In the *citation-sequence* system, each source is assigned a number the first time it is used in the text, and the same number identifies the source each time it appears. In the *citation-name* system, each source is assigned a number in the order in which it appears in the alphabetical list at the end of the paper. That number is used each time the source is cited in the text.

With all three systems, biologists place bibliographic information for each source at the end of the paper in a section called References or Cited References.

D2-f Sample student paper: Laboratory report

Conducting an experiment gives you practice in collecting and interpreting data. Writing a laboratory report allows you to describe an experiment and its results. The following laboratory report was written for a botany course. The writers used the style guidelines of the Council of Science Editors (CSE) for formatting their paper and citing and listing sources.

Distribution Pattern of Dandelion

(*Taraxacum officinale*)

on an Abandoned Golf Course

Marin Johnson

Laura Arnold

Lab 4

Botany 100A

Professor Ketchum

September 13, 2005

Title page consists of a descriptive title and the writers' names in the center of the page and the course, instructor, and date centered at the bottom of the page.

Marginal annotations indicate CSE-style formatting **and** effective writing.

Distribution Pattern of Dandelion 2

ABSTRACT

This paper reports our study of the distribution pattern of the common dandelion (*Taraxacum officinale*) at an abandoned golf course in Hilton, New York, on 10 July 2005. An area of 6 ha was sampled with 111 randomly placed 1×1 m^2 quadrats. The dandelion count from each quadrat was used to test observed frequencies against expected frequencies based on a hypothesized random distribution. We concluded that the distribution of dandelions was not random. We next calculated the coefficient of dispersion to test whether the distribution was aggregated (clumped) or uniform. The calculated value of this coefficient was greater than 1.0, suggesting that the distribution was aggregated. Such aggregated distributions are the most commonly observed types in natural populations.

INTRODUCTION

Theoretically, plants of a particular species may be aggregated (clumped), random, or uniformly distributed in space [1]. The distribution type may be determined by many factors, such as availability of nutrients, competition, distance of seed dispersal, and mode of reproduction [2].

The purpose of this study was to determine if the distribution pattern of the common dandelion (*Taraxacum officinale*) on an abandoned golf course was aggregated, random, or uniform.

METHODS

The study site was an abandoned golf course in Hilton, New York. The vegetation was predominantly grasses, along with dandelions, broad-leaf plantain (*Plantago major*), and bird's-eye speedwell (*Veronica chamaedrys*). We sampled an area of approximately 6 ha on 10 July 2005, approximately two weeks after the golf course had been mowed.

To ensure random sampling, we threw a tennis ball high in the air over the study area. At the spot where the tennis ball came to rest, we placed one corner of a 1×1 m^2 metal frame (quadrat). We then counted the number of dandelion plants within this quadrat. We repeated this procedure for a total of 111 randomly placed quadrats.

We used a two-step procedure [2]. We first tested whether the distribution of dandelion was random or nonrandom. From the counts of the number of dandelions in our 111 quadrats, we used a log-likelihood ratio

---

Margin notes:

An abstract summarizes the report in about 100–125 words. You may or may not be required to include an abstract with a brief lab report.

Introduction states the purpose of the experiment.

Citations are numbered in the order in which they appear in the text (citation-sequence style).

The writers use scientific names for plant species.

Detailed description of researchers' methods.

Distribution Pattern of Dandelion 3

(G) test to examine the goodness of fit between our observed frequencies and those expected based on the Poisson series $e^{-\mu}, \mu e^{-\mu}, \mu^2/2!e^{-\mu}, \mu^3/3!e^{-\mu}, \ldots$, where μ is the mean density of plants per quadrat. In carrying out this test, we grouped observed and expected frequencies so that no group had an expected frequency less than 1.0 [3]. We then determined whether the distribution was aggregated or uniform by calculating the coefficient of dispersion (ratio of the variance to the mean). A coefficient >1 indicates an aggregated distribution whereas a coefficient <1 indicates a more uniform distribution. Finally, we tested the significance of any departure of the ratio from a value of 1 by means of a *t*-test.

RESULTS

Table 1 shows the number of quadrats containing 0, 1, 2, . . . , 17 dandelion plants. More than two-thirds (67.6%) of the 111 quadrats contained no dandelion plants; almost 90% (89.2%) of the quadrats contained fewer than 3 dandelion plants. We observed a highly significant lack of fit between our observed frequencies and expected frequencies based on the Poisson distribution ($G = 78.4$, df $= 3$, $P < 0.001$). Thus, our data indicated that the distribution pattern of dandelion plants on the abandoned golf course was not random. The mean number of dandelion plants per quadrat was 1.05 (SD $= 2.50$), and the coefficient of dispersion was 5.95. A *t*-test showed that this value is significantly greater than 1.0 ($t = 36.7$, df $= 110$, $P < 0.001$), which strongly supports an aggregated distribution of the dandelion plants.

DISCUSSION

An aggregated (clumped) distribution is the most commonly observed distribution type in natural populations [4]. Among plants, aggregated distributions often arise in species that have poorly dispersed seeds or vegetative reproduction [2]. In the dandelion, the seeds are contained in light, parachute-bearing fruits that are widely dispersed by the wind. This method of seed dispersal would tend to produce a random distribution. However, dandelion plants also reproduce vegetatively by producing new shoots from existing taproots, and what we considered as groups of closely spaced

Page header contains an abbreviated title and the page number.

Specialized language of the field.

Headings organize the report into major sections.

Writers interpret their results and compare them with results of other researchers.

Distribution Pattern of Dandelion 4

Table presents the data collected by the researchers in an accessible format.

Table 1 Frequency distribution of dandelion *(Taraxacum officinale)* plants in $1 \times 1 \ m^2$ quadrats positioned randomly over 6 ha on an abandoned golf course

Number per quadrat	Observed frequency (f_i)	Expected frequency (f_i)[a]
0	75	38.68594
1	12	40.77707
2	12	21.49062
3	2	7.550757
4	3	1.989727
5	2	0.419456
6	0	0.073688
7	2	0.011096
8	0	0.001462
9	1	0.000171
10	0	1.8×10^{-5}
11	0	1.73×10^{-6}
12	0	1.52×10^{-7}
13	1	1.23×10^{-8}
14	0	9.27×10^{-10}
15	0	6.52×10^{-11}
16	0	4.29×10^{-12}
17	1	2.66×10^{-13}

Total 111

[a] Expected frequencies were calculated from the successive terms of the Poisson distribution (see Methods).

separate individuals probably represented shoots originating from the same plant. Thus, vegetative reproduction probably accounted for the observed aggregated distribution in this species.

REFERENCES

Sources are listed and numbered in the order in which they appear in the text.

1. Ketchum J. Lab manual for Botany 100; 2005.

2. Kershaw KA, Looney JHH. Quantitative and dynamic plant ecology. 3rd ed. London: Edward Arnold; 1985.

3. Zar JH. Biostatistical analysis. 5th ed. Englewood Cliffs (NJ): Prentice Hall; 2005.

4. Begon M, Harper JL, Townsend CR. Ecology: individuals, populations and communities. Oxford: Blackwell Science Limited; 1996.

D2-g Models of professional writing in the biological sciences

RESEARCH PAPER (EMPIRICAL STUDY)

Sponaugle S, Denit KL, Luthy SA, Serafy JE, Cowen RK. Growth variation in larval *Makaira nigricans*. Fish Biol. 2004;66:822-835.

LITERATURE REVIEW

Gesellchen V, Boutros M. Managing the genome: microRNAs in *Drosophila*. Differentiation. 2004;72:74-80.

RESEARCH PROPOSAL

Milner A. Development of a long-term ecological monitoring program at Denali National Park and Preserve as a prototype for national parks in the Subarctic: methods to classify streams using biotic communities for use in long-term ecological monitoring of stream ecosystems [Internet]. Anchorage (AK): Alaska Science Center; 2006 [cited 2006 Sep 27]; [6 p.]. Available from: http://www.absc.usgs.gov/research/Denali_USGS/downloads/agreements/Stream_Invertebrates_Research_Proposal.pdf

D3

Writing in business

Communication, especially writing, is central to the business world. Because business writers generally aim to persuade or inform their audiences, they place a premium on clarity, brevity, and focus. Business writers always take into account their audiences. If they are writing for their colleagues, for example, they may use a slightly less formal tone than if they are writing for clients or prospective clients. In all situations, business writers avoid complex metaphors and elaborate language; they also avoid slang and colloquial language.

When you write in business courses, you will usually write for a specific audience. Your goal will be to communicate in a straightforward manner and with a clear purpose.

D3-a Recognize the forms of writing in business.

In business courses, you will be asked to create documents that mirror the ones written in the field. The different forms of business writing covered in this section are used for varied purposes, such as informing and persuading. Assignments in business courses may include the following:

- reports
- proposals
- executive summaries
- memos and correspondence
- presentations
- brochures and newsletters

Reports

Reports present factual information for a variety of purposes. If your company is considering the development of a new product, you may be asked to write a feasibility report that lays out the pros and cons. If you are asked to determine how your sales compare with those of a competitor, you will need to write an investigative report. A progress report updates a client or supervisor about the status of a project. A formal report details a major project and generally requires research.

Proposals

Proposals are written with the goal of convincing a specific audience to adopt a plan. A solicited proposal is directed to an audience that has requested it. An unsolicited proposal is written for an audience that has not indicated interest. An internal proposal is directed at others in your organization. An external proposal is directed at clients or potential clients. The length of a proposal will vary depending on your goals and your intended audience.

Executive summaries

An executive summary provides a concise summary of the key points in a longer document, such as a proposal or a report, with the goal of drawing the reader's attention to the longer document.

Memos and correspondence

In business, communication often takes place via letter, memo, or e-mail. Letters and e-mail are written to clients, customers, and colleagues. Memos convey information to others in the same organization for a variety of purposes. A memo might summarize the results of a study or project, describe policies or standards, put forth a plan, or assign tasks.

Presentations

Presentations are usually done orally, in front of a group, to instruct, persuade, or inform. Presenters often use presentation software or tools such as whiteboards to prepare and display visuals — graphs, tables, charts, transparencies, and so on.

Brochures, newsletters, and Web sites

Brochures generally convey information about products or services to clients, donors, or consumers. Newsletters generally provide information about an organization to clients, members, or subscribers. Web sites may either advertise products or provide information about an organization.

D3-b Know the questions business writers ask.

In business, your purpose and your understanding of your audience will determine the questions you ask.

- If you are writing a proposal to persuade a client to adopt a product, you will ask, "How will this product benefit my client?" "What does my client need?"

- If you are asked to write a report informing your supervisor of your progress on a project, you will ask, "What does my supervisor need to know to authorize me to proceed?" You will also want to ask, "What does my supervisor already know?" "How can I target this report to address my supervisor's specific concerns?"

- If you are applying for a job, you will ask, "What qualifications do I have for this job?"

D3-c Understand the kinds of evidence business writers use.

In business, your purpose for writing, your audience, and the questions you ask will determine the type of evidence you use. The following are some examples of the way you might use evidence in business writing:

- If you are writing a report or a proposal, you may need to gather data through interviews, direct observation, surveys, or questionnaires. The sources of data you choose will be determined by your audience. For example, if you are studying the patterns of customer traffic at a supermarket to recommend a new layout, you might go to the supermarket and observe customers, or you might ask them to fill out surveys as they leave the store. If your audience is the store manager, you might focus on surveys at one store. If your audience is the owner of a large grocery chain, you would probably need to use data from several stores.

- If you are writing an investigative report in which you consider how to entice users to a health club, your evidence might include facts and statistics about the health benefits of exercise that you have drawn from published materials such as books, articles, and reports. You might also conduct research about the facilities of a competitor. In a long proposal or report, your evidence will probably come from a variety of sources rather than just one source.

- If you are applying for a job, your evidence will be your past experience and qualifications. For example, you might explain that you have worked in the industry for six years and held three management positions. You might also discuss how the skills you learned in those jobs will be transferable to the new position.

- If you are writing a brochure to promote a service, your evidence might be testimonials from satisfied users of the service. For example, a brochure advertising financial services might quote a customer who says, "My investments tripled after I took the advice of this company."

D3-d Become familiar with writing conventions in business.

In business, writing should be straightforward and professional, but not too formal.

- Buzzwords (*value-added, win-win, no-brainer*) and clichés (*The early bird catches the worm*) should be used sparingly. This kind of vocabulary is imprecise and can sound affected.

- Use personal pronouns such as *you* and *I*. Where appropriate (in letters, e-mails, proposals), you can use the pronoun *you* to emphasize the interests of your readers. When you are addressing multiple readers, you might want to avoid using *you* unless it is clear that you are referring to all readers. When you are expressing your opinion, you should use the pronoun *I*. When you are speaking on behalf of your company, you should use the pronoun *we*.

- In business writing, it is important to avoid language that could offend someone on the grounds of race, gender, sexual orientation, or disability. Use terms like *chair* or *chairperson* instead of *chairman* or *chairwoman* and *flight attendant* rather than *stewardess*. Unless it is relevant to your point, avoid describing people by race or ethnicity. If you are describing someone with a disability, use phrases like *client with a disability* rather than *disabled client* to show that you recognize the disability as one trait of the client rather than as something of overall importance. (Also see W4 in *A Writer's Reference*.)

- Business writing should always be concise. Avoid using words that are not essential to your point. For example, instead of writing *at this point in time*, just write *now*. Also avoid words that make a simple idea unnecessarily complicated. Using the passive voice often creates such complications. For example, instead of writing "This report was prepared to offer information to our customers," write "We prepared this report to inform our customers."

D3-e Use the APA or CMS (*Chicago*) system in business writing.

Business students typically use the style guidelines of the American Psychological Association (APA) or *The Chicago Manual of Style* (CMS) for formatting their paper, for citing sources in the text of their paper, and for listing sources at the end. The APA system is set forth in the *Publication Manual of the American Psychological Association*, 5th ed. (Washington: APA, 2001). CMS style is found in *The Chicago Manual of Style*, 15th ed. (Chicago: U of Chicago P, 2003). (For more details, see APA-4, APA-5, CMS-4, and CMS-5 in *A Writer's Reference*, Sixth Edition.) In business courses, instructors will usually indicate which style they prefer.

D3-f Sample student papers: An investigative report and a proposal

Sample report

Different business situations require different types of reports. Formal reports are comprehensive discussions of a topic from multiple angles, while investigative reports often focus on a specific issue. If you are asked to write a report, you should always be sure that you understand the expectations of your audience.

The investigative report beginning on page D-21 was written for an introductory course in business writing. The student, Brian Spencer, was asked to research the problem of employee motivation at a small company. He used the style guidelines of the American Psychological Association (APA) to format the paper and to cite and list sources.

Sample proposal

Proposals are written to convince a specific audience to adopt a plan. If you are asked to write a proposal, you might start by identifying the purpose and the audience for the document.

The internal proposal beginning on page D-28 was written for a course in business writing. The student, Kelly Ratajczak, wrote her proposal in the form of a memorandum to the senior vice president of human resources at the medium-sized company at which she was an intern. Her goal was to convince the vice president to adopt a wellness program for employees.

SAMPLE REPORT

Positively Affecting Employee Motivation

Prepared by Brian Spencer

Report Distributed March 9, 2006

Prepared for OAISYS

The title page of a business report is counted in the numbering, although a header and page number do not appear.

Title page of the report consists of the title, the writer's name, and the date in the center of the page and the company name centered at the bottom of the page.

Marginal annotations indicate business-style formatting and effective writing.

Page header contains an abbreviated title followed by five spaces and the page number. Preliminary pages (title page, abstract) use lowercase roman numerals; text pages use arabic numerals.

Abstract

Corporate goals, such as sales quotas or increases in market share, do not always take into account employee motivation. Motivating employees is thus a challenge and an opportunity for firms that want to outperform their competitors. For a firm to achieve its goals, its employees must be motivated to perform effectively.

Empirical research conducted with employees of a subject firm, OAISYS, echoed theories published by leading authorities in journals, books, and online reports. These theories argue that monetary incentives are not the primary drivers for employee motivation. Clear expectations, communication of progress toward goals, accountability, and public appreciation are common primary drivers. A firm aiming to achieve superior performance should focus on these activities.

Abstract, on a separate page, provides a brief summary of the report.

Employee Motivation   1

Introduction

All firms strive to maximize performance. Such performance is typically defined by one or more tangible measurements such as total sales, earnings per share, return on assets, and so on. The performance of a firm is created and delivered by its employees. Employees, however, are not necessarily motivated to do their part to maximize a firm's performance. Factors that motivate employees can be much more complex than corporate goals. This report will define the problem of employee motivation in one company and examine potential solutions.

OAISYS is a small business based in Tempe, Arizona, that manufactures business call recording products. Currently OAISYS employs 27 people. The business has been notably successful, generating annual compound sales growth of over 20% during the last three years. The company's management and board of directors expect revenue growth to accelerate over the coming three years to an annual compound rate of over 35%. This ambitious corporate goal will require maximum productivity and effectiveness from all employees, both current and prospective. OAISYS's management requested an analysis of its current personnel structure focused on the alignment of individual employee motivation with its corporate goal.

Background on Current Human Resources Program

OAISYS is currently structured departmentally by function. It has teams for research and development, sales, marketing, operations, and administration. Every employee has access to the same employment benefits, consisting of medical insurance, a 401(k) plan, flexible spending accounts, short- and long-term disability, and the like.

Members of the sales team receive a yearly salary, quarterly commissions tied to sales quotas, and quarterly bonuses tied to the

Introduction clearly presents the problem to be discussed and sets forth the scope of the report.

While not strictly APA style, the formatting of the business report is consistent with the style typically used in corporations. Headings are flush with the left margin and boldface. Paragraphs are separated by an extra line of space, and the first line of each paragraph is not indented.

Heading announces the purpose of each section.

 Writing in business

performance of specific tasks. These tasks can change quarterly to maintain alignment with strategic initiatives.

All employees not in the sales department receive a yearly salary and profit sharing at the end of the year. The formula for profit sharing is not known by the employees, and specific information about profits is infrequently communicated. When profitability is discussed, it is only in general terms. Key employees, as determined by the management, are given stock option grants periodically. This process is informal and very confidential.

Disconnect between Company and Employees

One common assumption is that a human resources program such as OAISYS's should be the platform for motivation. But monetary compensation is not the only driver of employee motivation (Dickson, 1973). In fact, studies have found that other factors are actually the primary drivers of employee motivation. Security, career advancement, the type of work, and pride in one's company are actually the highest rated factors in employee satisfaction (Accel TEAM, 2005).

Spencer presents evidence from research studies.

These conclusions drawn from the empirical research of others are supported by interviews conducted with current OAISYS employees. Justin Crandall, a current design engineer, stated that his primary motivation is the opportunity to work with leading-edge development tools to pursue results of the highest quality (personal communication, March 1, 2006). Crandall's strongest sense of frustration comes from a cluttered organizational structure because it restricts his ability to pursue innovative, high-quality results.

Spencer provides evidence from interviews with current employees.

Interviews are considered personal communication in APA style; they are cited in the text of the paper but not given in the reference list.

Todd Lindburg, the most senior design engineer on staff, had similar sentiments. His greatest motivator is the opportunity to create something lasting and important to the long-term success of the business (personal communication, March 2, 2006). Jack Wikselaar, vice president of sales, said he receives his strongest motivation from providing fulfilling job

Employee Motivation 3

opportunities for others (personal communication, March 3, 2006).

These findings of what motivates employees tell only half the story. Other research (*Motivating*, 2006) suggests that businesses can actually demotivate employees through certain behaviors, such as the following:

- company politics
- unclear expectations
- unnecessary rules and procedures
- unproductive meetings
- poor communication
- toleration of poor performance

A list draws readers' attention to important information.

Doug Ames, manager of operations for OAISYS, noted that some of these issues keep the company from outperforming expectations: "Communication is not timely or uniform, expectations are not clear and consistent, and some employees do not contribute significantly yet nothing is done" (personal communication, February 28, 2006).

Recommendations

It appears that a combination of steps can be used to unlock greater performance for OAISYS. Most important, steps can be taken to strengthen the corporate culture in key areas such as communication, accountability, and appreciation. Employee feedback indicates that these are areas of weakness or motivators that can be improved. This feedback is summarized in Figure 1.

The author lays out recommendations for action. Some reports also include a Conclusions section.

A plan to use communication effectively to set expectations, share results in a timely fashion, and publicly offer appreciation to specific contributors will likely go a long way toward aligning individual motivation with corporate goals. Additionally, holding individuals accountable for results will bring parity to the workplace.

One technique that might be effective is redefining compensation

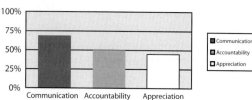

Graphic
illustrates
support for
the report's
key recom-
mendation.

Figure 1. Areas of greatest need for improvements in motivation.

to be based on specific responsibilities. Rather than tying
compensation to corporate profit, tying it to individual performance
will result in direct correlation between results and reward. Those
who do what is necessary to achieve expected results will be
rewarded. Those who miss the mark will be required to address the
reasons behind their performance and either improve or take a
different role. Professor of organizational behavior Jesper Sorenson
(2002) has noted that "quantitative analyses have shown that firms
with strong cultures outperform firms with weak cultures" (p. 70).
Taking steps to strengthen the corporate culture is critical to the
company's success.

Employee Motivation 5

References

Accel TEAM. (2005). *Employee motivation in the workplace.* Retrieved
March 2, 2006, from http://www.accel-team.com/motivation

Dickson, W. J. (1973). Hawthorne experiments. In C. Heyel (Ed.), *The
encyclopedia of management* (2nd ed., pp. 298-302). New York:
Van Nostrand Reinhold.

Motivating employees without money. (2006). Retrieved March 2,
2006, from http://www.employer-employee.com/howtomot.htm

Sorenson, J. B. (2002). The strength of corporate culture and the
reliability of firm performance. *Administrative Science Quarterly,
47*(1), 70-71.

Spencer
provides a
list of sources
using APA
style.

SAMPLE PROPOSAL

MEMORANDUM

Internal proposal is structured in memo format; subject identified in header.

To: Jay Crosson, Senior Vice President, Human Resources

From: Kelly Ratajczak, Intern, Purchasing Department

Subject: Proposal to Add a Wellness Program

Date: April 24, 2006

Ratajczak opens with a clear, concise statement of her main point.

Health care costs are rising. In the long run, implementing a wellness program in our corporate culture will decrease the company's health care costs.

Introductory section provides supporting background information.

Research indicates that nearly 70% of health care costs are from common illnesses related to high blood pressure, overweight, lack of exercise, high cholesterol, stress, poor nutrition, and other preventable health issues (Hall, 2006). Health care costs are a major expense for most businesses, and they do not reflect costs due to the loss of productivity or absenteeism. A wellness program would address most, if not all, of these health care issues and related costs.

Benefits of Healthier Employees

Not only would a wellness program substantially reduce costs associated with employee health care, but our company would prosper through many other benefits. Businesses that have wellness programs show a lower cost in production, fewer sick days, and healthier employees ("Workplace Health," 2006). Our healthier employees will help to cut not only our production and absenteeism costs but also potential costs such as higher turnover because of low employee morale.

Headings clearly define the sections of the proposal.

Implementing the Program

Implementing a good wellness program means making small changes to the work environment, starting with a series of information sessions. Simple changes to our work environment should include

Marginal annotations indicate business-style formatting and effective writing.

Wellness Program Proposal   2

Page header contains an abbreviated title followed by five spaces and an arabic page number. The first page of a memo is counted in the numbering, although a number does not appear.

healthier food selections in vending machines and in the employee cafeteria. A smoke-free environment, inside and outside the building, could be a new company policy. An important step is to educate our employees through information seminars and provide health care guides and pamphlets for work and home. In addition, the human resources department could expand the current employee assistance program by developing online materials that help employees and their families to assess their individual health goals.

Each health program is different in its own way, and there are a variety of programs that can be designed to meet the needs of our individual employees. Some programs that are becoming increasingly popular in the workplace are the following ("Workplace Health," 2006):

- health promotion programs
- subsidized health club membership
- return-to-work programs
- health-risk appraisals and screenings

Obstacles: Individual and Financial

Ratajczak identifies and responds to potential concerns.

The largest barrier in a wellness program is changing the habits and behaviors of our employees. Various incentives such as monetary bonuses, vacation days, merchandise rewards, recognition, and appreciation help to instill new habits and attitudes. Providing a healthy environment and including family in certain programs also help to encourage healthier choices and behaviors (Hall, 2006).

The costs of incorporating a wellness program will be far less than rising costs associated with health care in the long run. An employee's sense of recognition, appreciation, or accomplishment is an incentive that has relatively low or no costs. The owner of Natural Ovens Bakery, Paul Sitt, has stated that his company gained financially after providing programs including free healthy lunches for employees (Springer, 2005). Sitt said he believes that higher morale and keeping valuable employees have helped his business tremendously.

The concluding paragraph summarizes the main point, provides support for being competitive, and indicates a willingness to discuss the proposal.

It is important that our company be healthy in every way possible. Research shows that 41% of businesses already have some type of wellness program in progress and that 32% will incorporate programs within the next year ("Workplace Health," 2006). Our company should always be ahead of our competitors. I want to thank you for your time and I look forward to discussing this proposal with you further next week.

Ratajczak provides a list of the sources she used in her proposal. The reference list is formatted in APA style.

References

Hall, B. (2006). Good health pays off! Fundamentals of health promotion incentives. *Journal of Deferred Compensation 11*(2), 16-26. Retrieved April 17, 2006, from ProQuest database (975606661).

Springer, D. (2005, October 28). Key to business success? *La Crosse Tribune*. Retrieved April 17, 2006, from ProQuest database (920557951).

White, M. (2005). The cost-benefit of well employees. *Harvard Business Review, 83*(12), 22. Retrieved April 17, 2006, from ProQuest database (930371701).

Workplace health and productivity programs lower absenteeism, costs. (2006). *IOMA's report on managing benefit plans 6*(2), 1-4. Retrieved April 17, 2006, from ProQuest database (980950181).

D3-g Models of professional writing in business

REPORT

Public Safety Wireless Network Program. (2001, July). *Land mobile equipment market analysis report.* Retrieved August 25, 2006, from http://www.safecomprogram.gov/SAFECOM/library/technology/1176_landmobile.htm

REPORT FOR AN ACADEMIC AUDIENCE

Cable, D. M., Aiman-Smith, L., Mulvey, P. W., & Edwards, J. R. (2000). The sources and accuracy of job applicants' beliefs about organizational culture. *The Academy of Management Journal, 43*(6), 1076-1085.

NEWSLETTER

The Vitran Voice [Newsletter of the Vitran Corporation]. (2005). Retrieved August 29, 2006, from http://www.vitran.com/Corporation/PDF/winter2005.pdf

D4

Writing in education

The field of education draws on the knowledge and the methods of a variety of disciplines. As you study to become a teacher, you will take courses that focus on such diverse topics as the history of education, the psychology of teaching and learning, the development of curriculum, and instructional methods. You will also learn how to navigate classrooms and schools through both course work and field placements. Depending on what you plan to teach, you may also take courses in a specific content area (such as history or mathematics) or courses that focus on children with special needs. The writing you do in education courses will be designed to help you become a successful teacher.

D4-a Recognize the forms of writing in education.

Although there are many paths you can take as you train to become a teacher, you will encounter similar writing assignments in different courses. These may include the following:

- reflective essays, journals, and field notes
- curriculum designs and lesson plans
- reviews of instructional materials
- case studies
- research papers
- self-evaluations
- portfolios

Reflective essays, journals, and field notes

Much of the writing you do in education courses will encourage you to reflect on your own attitudes, beliefs, and experiences and how they inform your thoughts about teaching and learning. In an introductory course, for example, you may be asked to write an essay in which you reflect on your own education in the context of a theory that you are studying. As a field observer or student teacher, you may be asked to keep a journal or notes in which you reflect on your interaction with students, teacher-student interactions, student-student interactions, diversity issues, and student progress. These reflections might then serve as the basis for an essay in which you connect your experiences to course content.

Curriculum designs and lesson plans

In some courses, especially those focused on teaching methods, you will be asked to design individual lessons or units in a particular content area. In an early childhood education course, for example, you might be asked to read several children's books and write a plan for a class activity that is related to the books. In a science methods course, you might be asked to design a unit about plant biology. In a methods course for special education, you might be asked to design an individualized education plan for a specific student. For any of these courses, you might also be asked to integrate technology into your curriculum design.

Reviews of instructional materials

In a review of materials, you assess the value of a set of instructional materials for classroom use. For example, you might be asked to look at several textbooks and explain which would be most useful in a particular classroom setting.

Case studies

Some education courses require students to conduct and write case studies. Case studies may involve observation and analysis of an individual student, a teacher, or classroom interactions. The goal of a case study may be to determine how the process of teaching or learning takes place or how an event can illuminate something about learning or classroom dynamics.

Research papers

In some education courses, you might be assigned papers that focus on broader educational issues or problems and that require you to conduct research and then formulate your own ideas about the topic. In a course about the history of education, you might be asked to research the evolution of literacy in the United States. In a developmental psychology course, you might be asked to research how students learn mathematics.

Self-evaluations

As a teacher candidate, you will be asked to evaluate your own teaching and learning. The format of the self-evaluation will vary depending on whether you are evaluating yourself as a learner or as a teacher. Sample questions of self-evaluation as a teacher may include the following:

- What were the strengths and weaknesses of your lesson or unit plan?
- How did your lesson further student learning?
- What have you learned about yourself and your students from teaching this class?
- How can you improve your teaching?

Portfolios

Most teacher education programs require you to assemble a teaching portfolio before you graduate. The purpose of the portfolio is to provide information about your teaching experience and your teaching philosophy. The contents of portfolios vary, but common documents include a statement of teaching philosophy, a statement of professional goals, a résumé, evaluations, and sample course materials. Education departments at some institutions will require you to assemble an electronic portfolio as well as a print version.

D4-b Know the questions educators ask.

Educators ask questions that are practical, theoretical, and self-reflective. Practical questions tend to focus on classroom and curriculum issues such as student progress and implementation of new approaches. Theoretical questions focus on how students should be educated and on the intellectual, political, and social contexts of learning. Self-reflective questions allow for discussion of the teacher's own role in the educational process. Any of the following questions could form the basis for a paper in an education course:

- How does this school's language arts curriculum prepare students to be information-literate?
- What are the effects of the use of standardized tests in economically disadvantaged districts in comparison with more affluent districts?
- How do my perceptions of my own education influence the way I approach teaching?

D4-c Understand the kinds of evidence educators use.

Educators and education students rely on evidence that is both quantitative (statistics, survey results, test scores) and qualitative (case studies, observation, personal experience). The following are some examples of evidence used in different situations:

- If you are writing a research paper that compares different approaches to social studies education, you might rely on quantitative evidence such as the results of standardized tests from different school districts.
- For a paper on child development, you might use a combination of personal observation and evidence from published case studies.
- If you are keeping a journal of your student teaching experiences, your evidence would come from your experiences in the classroom and from the changes in your attitudes over time.
- If you are creating a lesson plan, you will focus on your teaching objectives and explain how your plan will achieve those objectives.

D4-d Become familiar with writing conventions in education.

Educators agree on several conventions when they write:

- The personal pronoun *I* is commonly used in reflective writing.

- Research papers and case studies are generally written in the third person (*he, she, it, they*) and in a more formal, objective tone.

- Educators have a specialized vocabulary that includes terms such as *pedagogy* (teaching principles and methods), *practice* (actual teaching), *curriculum* (the written lesson plans followed by a class or school), *assessment* (the determination of whether students or teachers are successful), *achievement tests* (tests that measure what students have learned), and *NCLB* (the No Child Left Behind Act). You will likely use such terms in your writing.

Because the field of education draws on various disciplines, including psychology, history, and sociology, it is important to be aware of writing conventions in those disciplines as well. (See D5 and D7.)

D4-e Use the APA or CMS (*Chicago*) system in writing in education.

Writers in education typically use the style guidelines of the American Psychological Association (APA) or *The Chicago Manual of Style* (CMS) for formatting their paper, for citing sources in the text of their paper, and for listing sources at the end. The APA system is set forth in the *Publication Manual of the American Psychological Association*, 5th ed. (Washington: APA, 2001). CMS style is found in *The Chicago Manual of Style*, 15th ed. (Chicago: U of Chicago P, 2003). (For more details, see APA-4, APA-5, CMS-4, and CMS-5 in *A Writer's Reference*, Sixth Edition.) In education courses, instructors will usually indicate which style they prefer.

D4-f Sample student paper: Reflective essay

In some education courses, you may be asked to write reflective essays in which you describe and analyze your own attitudes, beliefs, and experiences. Some reflective essays focus solely on personal observations while others integrate ideas from other sources as well.

The following reflective essay was written for a service learning course in which students explored issues of diversity, power, and opportunity in school settings. The writer, Onnalee Gibson, used a variety of professional sources to inform her own ideas about her experiences working with an eleventh-grade student. She formatted her paper and cited and listed her sources following the guidelines of the American Psychological Association (APA).

Service Learning: Eric   i

Page header contains an abbreviated title followed by five spaces and the page number. Preliminary pages such as the title page are numbered with lowercase roman numerals.

A Reflection on Service Learning:

Working with Eric

Descriptive title is centered on the page; the writer's name, the course, the instructor, and the date are centered at the bottom of the page.

Onnalee L. Gibson

Teacher Education 250

Professor Carter

April 25, 2006

Marginal annotations indicate APA-style formatting and effective writing.

D4-f Writing in education

Text pages are
numbered with
arabic numerals.

The first time I saw the beautiful yet simple architecture of
Waverly High School, I was enchanted. I remember driving by while
exploring my new surroundings as a transfer student to Michigan
State University and marveling at the long front wall of reflective
windows, the shapely bushes, and the general cleanliness of the

Reflective essays
may include
descriptive
passages.

school grounds. When I was assigned to do a service learning project
in a local school district, I hoped for the opportunity to find out
what it would be like to work at a school like Waverly--a school
where the attention to its students' needs was evident from the
outside in.

Waverly High School, which currently enrolls about 1,100
students in grades 9 through 12 and has a teaching staff of 63, is

Background in-
formation about
the school sets
the scene for
Gibson's personal
experiences.

extremely diverse in several ways. Economically, students range from
poverty level to affluent. Numerous ethnic and racial groups are
represented. And in terms of achievement, the student body boasts
an assortment of talents and abilities.

The school provides a curriculum that strives to meet the
needs of each student and uses a unique grade reporting system that
itemizes each aspect of a student's grade. The system allows both
teachers and parents to see where academic achievement and
academic problems surface. Unlike most schools, which evaluate
students on subjects in one number or letter grade, Waverly has a
report card that lists individual grades for tests, homework, exams,
papers, projects, participation, community service, and attendance.
Thus, if a student is doing every homework assignment and is still
failing tests, this breakdown of the grades may effectively highlight
how the student can be helped.

Transition leads
from background
information
about the
school to
Gibson's personal
experiences.

It was this unique way of evaluating students that led to my
first meeting with Eric Johnson, an 11th grader to whom I was
assigned as a tutor. Eric is an African American male who grew up in
a nuclear middle-class family in a Lansing suburb. Teachers noticed
over time that Eric's grades were dropping, yet his attendance,
participation, and motivation were above average. Surprisingly, Eric
himself was the one who asked for a tutor to help him raise his
grades. What initially struck me about Eric was the level of

Service Learning: Eric   2

responsibility he seemed to take for his own academic achievement. At the time I wrote in my journal (January 31, 2006), "He appears to be a good student. He is trying his best to succeed in school. *He came to me for help and realizes the need for a tutor.*"

While tutoring Eric, I paid attention to the way he talked about his classes and to the types of assignments he was being asked to complete. My impression was that Waverly High School was fostering student success by doing more than just placing posters in the hallways. Waverly's curriculum encourages analytical thinking, requires group and individual projects that depend on creativity and research, and includes open-ended writing assignments designed to give students opportunities to form their own conclusions. I found this reality both difficult and inspiring; I had not expected an 11th grader's homework to be so challenging. I once said so to Eric, and he responded with a smile: "Yeah. My teachers say it's going to help us when we get to college to already know how to do some of these things." What was surprising to me was the faculty's collective assumption that high school was not the end of a student's career. The fact that teachers talk with students about what will be expected *when* (not *if*) they go to college is significant. That kind of positive language, which I heard many times at Waverly, most certainly affects students' sense of themselves as achievers. In this case, Eric was not preoccupied with worrying about whether he wanted to go to college or would be accepted; rather, he mentally prepared himself for the time when he would actually enroll.

According to education researcher Jean Anyon (1981), "Students from higher social class backgrounds may be exposed to legal, medical, or managerial knowledge . . . while those of the working classes may be offered a more 'practical' curriculum" (p. 5). I do not see this gravitation toward social reproduction holding true for most students at Waverly High School. Waverly's student body is a mix of social classes, yet the school's philosophy is to push each of its students to consider college. Through its curriculum, its guidance department literature, and its opportunities for career field trips, Waverly is opening doors for all of its students. In Eric's case, I

Journal entries are considered personal communication and are cited in the text but not included in the reference list.

Personal observations lead to broader insights.

Gibson analyzes her evidence to draw a broader conclusion.

This section bridges academic theory and personal experience.

also observed the beginnings of a break in social reproduction. From the start of our tutoring sessions, Eric frequently mentioned that neither of his parents went to college (Gibson, journal entry, March 14, 2006). This made me wonder how his parents talk to him about college. Is the desire to go to college something they have instilled in him? Have they given him the message that if he works hard and goes to college he will be successful? If that is the case, then Eric's parents are attempting to break the cycle with their children--and they have the good fortune to live in a school district that supports their desires. In contrast to the idea that most people have nothing more than social reproduction to thank for their socioeconomic status (Bowles & Gintis, 1976), Eric seems to believe that hard work and a college education are keys to his success.

Another key to Eric's success will be the resources he enjoys as a student at Waverly. Abundance of or lack of resources can play an important part in students' opportunities to learn and succeed. Because nearly half of all school funding comes from local property taxes (D. Carter, class lecture, April 4, 2006), areas with smaller populations or low property values do not have the tax base to fund schools well. As a result, one education finance expert has argued, some children receive substandard education (Parrish, 2002). Waverly does not appear to have serious financial or funding issues. Each student has access to current textbooks, up-to-date computer labs, a well-stocked library, a full art and music curriculum, and numerous extracurricular activities. While countless schools are in desperate need of a better equipped library, Waverly's library has a rich collection of books, magazines and journals, computer stations, and spaces in which to use all of these materials. It is a very user-friendly library. This has shown me what the power of funding can do for a school. Part of Waverly's (and its students') success results from the ample resources spent on staff and curriculum materials. Adequate school funding is one of the factors that drive school and student success.

Aside from funding, placement policies determine school and student success. A major concern of both educators and critics of

Margin notes:

Source is cited in APA in-text citation style.

Class lecture (personal communication) is cited in the text only, not in the reference list.

Gibson considers the larger implications of her personal observations.

education policies is that schools will place students into special education programs unnecessarily. Too often students who do not need special education are coded for special ed--even when they have a learning issue that can be handled with a good teacher in a mainstream class (D. Carter, class lecture, April 6, 2006). At Waverly High School, teachers and counselors are not so quick to shuffle Eric into special ed. I agree with several of Eric's teachers who feel that he may have a mild learning disability. I began to feel this way when Eric and I moved from working in a private tutoring space to working in the library. It was clear to me that he had difficulty paying attention in a public setting. On February 9, I wrote in my journal:

> Eric was extremely distracted. He couldn't pay attention to what I was asking, and he couldn't keep his eyes on his work. There were other students in the library today, and he kept eavesdropping on their conversations and shaking his head when they said things he did not agree with. This is how he must behave in the classroom; he is easily distracted but he wants to work hard. I see that it is not so much that he needs a tutor because he can't understand what his teachers are telling him; it is more that he needs the one-on-one attention in a confined room free of distractions.

Even though Eric showed signs of distraction, I never felt as if he should be coded for special education. I am pleased that the administration and learning specialists did not decide to place Eric in a special education track. Eric is exceedingly intelligent and shows promise in every academic area. He seems to be able to succeed by identifying problems on his own and seeking resources to help him solve those problems. He is a motivated and talented student who simply seems like a typical adolescent.

I came away from my service learning project with an even stronger conviction about the importance of quality education for a student's success. Unlike the high school I attended, Waverly pays close attention to each child and thinks about how to get all its students to succeed at their own level. Jean Patrice, an administrator, told me, "You have to be able to reach a student where *they* are instead of making them come to you. If you don't, you'll lose them" (personal communication, April 10, 2006). Patrice expressed her desire to see all students get something out of their educational experience. This feeling is common among members of Waverly's faculty. With such a positive view of student potential, it is no wonder that 97% of Waverly High School graduates go on to a four-year university (Patrice). I have no doubt that Eric Johnson will attend college and that he will succeed there.

As I look toward my teaching future, I know there is plenty that I have left to learn. Teaching is so much more than getting up in front of a class, reiterating facts, and requiring students to learn a certain amount of material by the end of the year. Teaching is about getting students--one by one--to realize and act on their potential. This course and this service learning experience have made me realize that we should never have a trial-and-error attitude about any student's opportunities and educational quality.

Second citation to the same source in one paragraph requires only a name.

Conclusion raises questions for further reflection.

Service Learning: Eric   6

References

Anyon, J. (1981). Social class and school knowledge. *Curriculum
    Inquiry, 11*(1), 5.

Bowles, S., & Gintis, H. (1976). *Schooling in capitalist America:
    Educational reform and contradictions of economic life.* New
    York: Basic Books.

Parrish, T. (2002). Racial disparities in identification, funding, and
    provision of special education. In D. Losen & G. Orfield (Eds.),
    Racial inequity in special education. Cambridge, MA: Civil Rights
    Project and Harvard Education Press.

List of references uses APA style.

List is alphabetized by authors' last names.

Double-spacing is used throughout.

D4-g Models of professional writing in education

RESEARCH PAPER

Seitsinger, A. M. (2005). Service-learning and standards-based instruction in middle schools. *Journal of Educational Research, 99*(1), 19-30.

CASE STUDY

Wang, J., & Odell, S. J. (2003). Learning to teach toward standards-based writing instruction: Experiences of two preservice teachers and two mentors in an urban multicultural classroom. *The Elementary School Journal, 104*(2), 147-174.

LESSON PLAN

Alejandre, S. (2006). What is area? Retrieved November 1, 2006, from http://mathforum.org/alejandre/frisbie/one.inch.tiles.html

D5

Writing in history

Historians analyze the information available to them to develop their own theories about past events, experiences, ideas, and movements. Depending on their interests, historians may consider a variety of issues and sources, including those related to economics, politics, social issues, science, the military, gender, the family, and popular culture. Historians do not simply record what happened at a particular time; rather, they attempt to explain *why* or *how* events occurred as they did and to place those events in a larger context. For example, a historical study of women in the British military during World War II would not simply describe the positions women held in the armed forces; through an analysis of the available information, it might develop a theory about why women were authorized to hold certain jobs and not others and how changes to women's roles affected the evolution of the women's rights movement in the decades that followed.

Historians write either for an audience of students and other scholars or for a general audience of interested readers. When you write for history courses, you will most likely address other students of history. Your challenge—and the challenge to every historian—is to consider yourself part of an ongoing discussion with other scholars and to place your own ideas in the context of existing interpretations.

D5-a Recognize the forms of writing in history.

Writing in history combines narrative (a description of what happened) and interpretation (an analysis of why events occurred). Historians ask questions that do not have obvious answers and analyze a variety of sources to draw conclusions.

When you take courses in history you may be asked to write any of the following kinds of documents:

- critical essays
- book reviews
- research papers
- historiographic essays

Critical essays

For some assignments, you will be asked to write a short, critical essay in which you look at a document or group of documents—or perhaps a historical argument written by a scholar. For example, if you were studying the US decision to send troops to Vietnam, you might be asked to analyze one or more of John F. Kennedy's speeches and put forth a theory about why Kennedy chose to authorize the initial troop deployments. In the same course, you might be asked to read a journal article by a scholar analyzing Kennedy's decision and assess the way that scholar used evidence to support his or her conclusion.

Book reviews

Because historians view their own work as part of an ongoing scholarly conversation, they value the serious discussion of the work of other scholars in the field. In some courses, you may be asked to write a book review in which you analyze the logic and accuracy of a scholarly work or several works on the same topic. When you write a book review, you will have to make judgments about how much background information to provide about the book so that your readers will be able to understand and appreciate your critique.

Research papers

When you write a research paper in any course, you are expected to pose a question and examine the available evidence to find an answer to that question. In history courses, a research paper will generally focus on *why* and *how* questions that can be answered using a combination of sources. If you were studying the Vietnam War, you might be curious about how the rhetoric of the cold war shaped John F. Kennedy's early Vietnam policy. To answer this question, you might look at government documents from the Kennedy administration, press coverage of Kennedy's foreign policy, Kennedy's own writings, and interviews with those who were involved in policy making. If you were interested in the role of women in the military during World War II, you might ask why the British government supported the expansion of women's roles in ways that the US government did not.

Historiographic essays

Historiography is the study by historians of how history is written. When you write a historiographic essay, you think about the methods by which other historians have drawn their conclusions. If you were writing a historiographic essay about how the cold war affected John F. Kennedy's policies, you would analyze how other historians have answered this question. What assumptions or biases influenced their choice and interpretation of sources? What methods shaped their work?

D5-b Know the questions historians ask.

Historians generally ask *how* and *why* questions. Other, more basic questions such as "What happened?" and "Who was involved?" will contribute to the answers to the broader, more controversial questions. Historians choose their questions by considering their own interests, the relevance to the ongoing discussions among scholars, and the availability of sources on the topic. The answer to any one of the following questions could form the basis of a thesis for a history paper:

- Why did John F. Kennedy decide to send American troops to Vietnam?
- Why did Congress decide to grant women the vote?
- How did the institution of a minimum wage affect the middle class?
- Why did the Roman Empire collapse?

D5-c Understand the kinds of evidence historians use.

As investigators of the past, historians rely on both primary sources and secondary sources. Primary sources are materials from the historical period being studied—government documents, numerical data, speeches, diaries, letters, and maps. Secondary sources are materials produced after the historical period that interpret or synthesize historical events. The same source can function as either a primary or a secondary source depending on what you are writing about. For example, a newspaper article about John F. Kennedy's decision to send troops to Vietnam would be a secondary source in an essay about why Kennedy made this decision. The same article, however, would be a primary source in an essay about newspaper coverage of Kennedy's presidency.

Following are some of the ways historians use evidence:

- For a research paper about the role of women in the British military during World War II, you might find evidence in women's diaries and letters. If you were interested in how the government decided to create women's military services, you could consult records of parliamentary debates or correspondence between military or government leaders. You could also find numerous books by other scholars with information on this topic.

- For a research paper about attitudes toward Prohibition in different parts of the United States, you might consult regional newspapers or correspondence between politicians and their constituents. You might also find numerical data on liquor sales and Prohibition violations to support a hypothesis about regional attitudes.

- For a review of several books about the fall of the Roman Empire, your evidence would come from the books themselves as well as other respected sources on the topic.

D5-d Become familiar with writing conventions in history.

No matter what topic they are writing about, historians agree on a set of general conventions:

- Historians value counterargument. To draw a conclusion about why or how something happened, historians must weigh conflicting theories and interpretations carefully and judiciously. In an essay answering the question of why Congress passed the Nineteenth Amendment, you might conclude that politicians truly believed that women should have the right to vote. But you would also need to account for the failure of the same legislation several years earlier. Did politicians change their minds? Or were other factors at work?

- Historians conduct research. Historians, like detectives or forensic specialists, look for explanations by assessing the available evidence rather than relying on assumptions or personal opinions. They look for multiple sources of evidence to confirm their theories, and they avoid value judgments.

- Historians write in the past tense. Although historians consider their work relevant to the understanding of current events, they focus on past events, ideas, and movements and indicate this focus by using the past tense.

- Historians credit the scholarship of others. Historians are aware that they are joining an existing scholarly conversation, and they place great importance on citing the ideas of other scholars.

D5-e Use the CMS (*Chicago*) system in writing in history.

Writers in history typically use the style guidelines of *The Chicago Manual of Style* (CMS) for formatting their papers, for citing sources in the text of their paper and in endnotes, and for listing sources in a bibliography at the end. CMS style is set forth in *The Chicago Manual of Style*, 15th ed. (Chicago: U of Chicago P, 2003). (For more details, see CMS-4 and CMS-5 in *A Writer's Reference*, Sixth Edition.)

D5-f Sample student paper: Research essay (excerpt)

A history research paper generally focuses on a *how* or a *why* question, and it answers this question with an analysis of available sources. The student paper excerpted beginning on page D-49 was written for a course on the history of the industrial revolution in the United States. The student, Jenna Benjamin, used the style guidelines of *The Chicago Manual of Style* (CMS) to format her paper and to cite and list her sources.

Wage Slavery or True Independence?

Women Workers in the Lowell, Massachusetts,

Textile Mills, 1820-1850

Jenna Benjamin

American History 200, Section 4

Professor Jones

May 22, 2006

Title page consists of a descriptive title and the writer's name in the center of the page and the course number, instructor, and date at the bottom of the page.

Marginal annotations indicate CMS-style formatting and effective writing.

Page header
contains the
writer's name
followed by the
page number.
Since the title
page is counted
in the number-
ing, the first
text page is
numbered 2.

Introduction
frames a debat-
able issue.

Research ques-
tions focus the
essay.

Statement of
thesis.

Section pro-
vides back-
ground about
the historical
period.

Historians write
in the past
tense when
describing past
events.

In 1813, Francis Lowell introduced a new type of textile mill to
Massachusetts that would have a permanent impact on family and
village life by speeding the transformation of the home production
system to one of factory production. Over the next three decades,
this new system of production would require a substantial labor force
and would lead to the unprecedented hiring of thousands of women.
The entrance of young women into the workforce sparked a
passionate debate about whether factory work exploited young
women and whether allowing them into the workforce would have a
negative impact on society. Indeed, the young women who went to
Lowell worked for low pay and had little free time. Were these
women victims of the factory system? What was the long-term
impact of their experiences? An analysis of the available evidence
reveals that rather than being exploited, these women workers
shaped their experience for their own purposes, actively engaging in
expanding the constricted opportunities for women.

Until the early nineteenth century, the vast majority of
Americans grew up in farm families. As the industrial revolution
spread across England, rural Americans felt certain that the dark and
dreary factory towns that were beginning to dot the English
countryside would not arise in America. News coming from England
contained reports that a permanent class of exploited workers was
being created there. America, with its commitment to opportunity,
would not, people were sure, experience such a fate. New England
had been in the forefront of the struggle against British rule. Rural
people in that region were especially proud of their independence
and suspicious of anything that seemed to copy the ways of the
English.[1]

New Englanders watched the rise of industrialization in
England with concern. Changes in production there were most
noticeable in the making of cloth. As late as the 1760s, English
textile merchants were still making cloth by the age-old "putting
out" system. They bought raw wool and hired women to spin it at
home. When the wool had been spun into yarn, the merchants then
sent it to weavers, who also worked in their homes. In the 1760s,

Benjamin 3

however, new machinery (the carding cylinder, the spinning jenny, and, most important, the water frame) was developed that made possible the shift of spinning and weaving from homes to what were called "factories." By 1800, many such factories had been established in England, usually employing children to do most of the work. Many of these children were orphans or "paupers" from families so poor that they could not even afford to feed them. Conditions in the factories were very bad, and stories of dark and dangerous mills (some accurate, some exaggerated) found their way to America and reinforced the prejudice against England and industry.[2]

The economy of New England early in the nineteenth century was tied to commerce and agriculture, not industry. The wealth of New England merchants had been made in foreign trade, and few of them saw the need to turn to other pursuits. Some worried that the development of American manufactures would diminish the need to import foreign goods. Until the War of 1812, which cut the United States off from trade in English goods, most wealthy merchants in the Northeast were content to stay in the business that had made their riches.[3] Moreover, where would American factory workers come from? England had a large class of peasants who served as a pool of potential factory labor. In America, however, when land wore out or harvests were poor, Yankee farmers could move west to the vast territories being taken from Native Americans.

While great changes in the production of textiles were taking place in England, most New Englanders still spun yarn at home and some also wove their own cloth. In most cases they were simply making clothes for their families. Much of this work was done by women. A spinning wheel was a possession of almost every household.[4] Despite their anti-industrial prejudice, however, New England farmers witnessed, in the first two decades of the nineteenth century, a slow shift in the way cloth was made in America. Home production gradually gave way to "putting out," and that system was eventually replaced by factory production. Why did this change occur?

Unlike most merchants in America, a few, like Samuel Slater

Benjamin raises a question that she will answer using evidence from primary and secondary sources.

and Francis Cabot Lowell, were impressed by the mechanization of English textile production and began to think about an American textile industry. Men like these noted the massive increase in productivity in the English textile industry. At first, Slater and others who followed his lead built small mills in rural villages and employed not children as in England but whole families. The building of Slater-type mills did not directly challenge the New England way of living. Most villages already contained small mills run by water power (streams pushing paddle wheels) that ground corn or wheat. Since the textile mills hired whole families who already lived in the villages, family and village life was not greatly altered.[5]

Transition to new section of paper.

One new development in textile production, however, did raise troublesome questions about the impact of industrialization on America's rural way of life. This change came from a new machine, the power loom, and a new type of mill. The first mill of its type was built in Waltham, Massachusetts, in 1813 by Francis Lowell and a small group of wealthy Boston merchants.[6] Three years earlier, Lowell had returned from a long trip to England. The British government would not allow the plans for its new power looms to be taken out of the country, but Lowell had paid close attention to their construction on his tours of English mills and returned to America with enough knowledge to eventually reproduce a machine comparable to the English power loom.[7]

In Waltham, Francis Lowell built a large mill that carried out both the spinning and the weaving processes. Every step of the production process was done in a series of connected steps. Waltham was not a village with a textile mill in it; it was a "mill town" in which the factory dominated the economic life of a rapidly growing city. Most significantly, Lowell's system of production brought important changes in the lives of his workers. He hired them as individuals, not as families, and many came from great distances to live and work in the new mill town. When Lowell died in 1817, the small group of Boston businessmen who had invested in his mill at Waltham spread the new factory system to other places. Their biggest investment was in the small village of East Chelmsford, about

Benjamin 5

twenty-seven miles from Boston and lying along the swift-flowing
Concord and Merrimack Rivers. There they built what was soon the
biggest mill town in the nation, with more than a dozen large
integrated mills using mechanical looms. In honor of their friend,
they called the new town Lowell.[8] (See Figure 1 for a map of Lowell
in 1845.)

A primary
source (a map) is
included in the
paper.

　　The growth of Lowell between 1821 and 1840 was
unprecedented.[9] A rapidly developing textile industry like the one at
Lowell needed more and more people to work the mechanical looms
and other machines in the factories. Given the prejudice against
factory work in New England, how could large numbers of natives be
drawn to work in the mills? It was a question that had been carefully

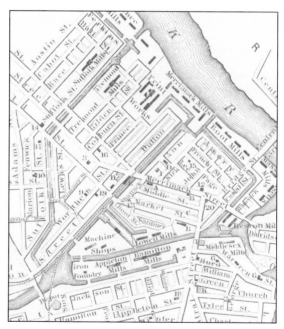

Figure 1. Detail of map of Lowell, Massachusetts, 1845, showing mill
buildings along the Merrimack River. (Lowell Historical Society.)

pondered by the wealthy men who built the big textile mills at
Lowell, Massachusetts.

The mill owners, aware of the negative view of English mill
towns, decided to confront the problem by creating a *planned*
community where workers would live in solid, clean housing rather
than slums. Their source of workers would also be different. The
rapidly running rivers that ran their mills were not near the major
coastal cities. No large pool of potential laborers lived near their
new town. The mill owners had to find a large group of people whose
labor was not absolutely necessary to the farm economy. The
solution to their labor problem came in the form of hundreds (later
thousands) of young women who lived on the farms of the region.[10]

Several developments in the social and economic history of
New England tended to make this group of workers available.
Population growth was making it more and more difficult for farmers
to find land close by for their sons (and their sons' families).
Generations of the same family had hoped to live near one another.
By the 1820s, however, many farms in New England, especially those
on the less productive land of Maine and New Hampshire, had run
out of good land and needed to find sources of income outside of
agriculture. While some farmers went west to find more fertile land
and a less harsh climate, others sent their sons to work on
neighboring farms or as apprentices to craftsmen (shoemakers,
blacksmiths, or leather workers). Extra cash was something that most
farm families were in great need of.[11]

Another factor helped set the stage for the successful
industrialization of textile production. This one was within the
structure of the family itself and worked in favor of producing a new
group of workers for the mills. The position of women (wives and,
especially, daughters) in the family was an inferior one. Adult,
property-holding males were citizens with full civil rights, but the
same was not true for women *of any age*. The father of the family
had the legal right to control most aspects of the lives of his wife
and daughters. His wife could own no property. Her signature on a

Benjamin cites
secondary
sources, two
books written
about the period.

Writer further
develops the
answers to
her research
questions.

Benjamin 16

Notes

1. Caroline F. Ware, *The Early New England Cotton Manufacture* (Boston: Houghton Mifflin, 1931), 4-8; Barbara M. Tucker, *Samuel Slater and the Origins of the American Textile Industry: 1790-1860* (Ithaca: Cornell University Press, 1984), 38-41; Robert F. Dalzell, *Enterprising Elite: The Boston Associates and the World They Made* (Cambridge, MA: Harvard University Press, 1987), 12-13; Jonathan Prude, *The Coming of Industrial Order: Town and Factory Life in Rural Massachusetts, 1810-1860* (Cambridge: Cambridge University Press, 1983), 6-12; Allan Kulikoff, "The Transition to Capitalism in Rural America," *William and Mary Quarterly* 46, no. 1 (1989): 129-30, 141-42.

2. Tucker, *Samuel Slater,* 33-40.

3. Dalzell, *Enterprising Elite*, 41-42; Ware, *Cotton Manufacture*, 3-8, 62.

4. Thomas Dublin, *Women at Work: The Transformation of Work and Community in Lowell, Massachusetts, 1826-1860* (New York: Columbia University Press, 1979), 14; Adrienne D. Hood, "The Gender Division of Labor in the Production of Textiles in Eighteenth-Century Rural Pennsylvania," *Journal of Social History* 27 (Spring 1994), http://www.searchbank.com/infotrac/session/4/0/82904/37xrn_7.

5. Tucker, *Samuel Slater,* 79, 85, 99-100, 111; Barbara M. Tucker, "The Family and Industrial Discipline in Ante-Bellum New England," *Labor History* 21 (Winter 1979-80): 56-60.

6. Dalzell, *Enterprising Elite*, 26-30; Tucker, *Samuel Slater,* 111-16.

7. Dalzell, *Enterprising Elite*, 5-6.

8. Tucker, *Samuel Slater,* 116-17.

9. Dublin, *Women at Work*, 19-21, 133-35.

10. Ibid., 26, 76; Benita Eisler, ed., *The "Lowell Offering": Writings by New England Mill Women, 1840-1845* (Philadelphia: Lippincott, 1977), 15-16.

11. Christopher Clark, "The Household Economy: Market Exchange and the Rise of Capitalism in the Connecticut Valley, 1800-1860," *Journal of Social History* 13 (Winter 1979): 175-76; Gail Fowler Mohanty, "Handloom Outwork and Outwork Weaving in Rural Rhode Island, 1810-1821," *American Studies* 30 (Fall 1989): 42-43, 48-49.

Endnotes begin on a new page.

Secondary sources—books, articles, Web sites—are cited in endnotes in CMS (*Chicago*) style. Complete source information is also listed in the bibliography.

Citation of a Web source.

Second reference to a source includes the author's name, a shortened title, and the page numbers.

Benjamin 19

Bibliography
begins on a
new page and
includes all the
sources the
writer cites in
the paper.

Entries are
listed alphabeti-
cally by authors'
last names or
by title for
works with no
author.

First line of
each entry is at
the left margin;
subsequent
lines are in-
dented ½"
(or five spaces).

Bibliography

Bartlett, Elisha. *A Vindication of the Character and Condition of the Females Employed in the Lowell Mills.* 1841. Reprinted in *Women of Lowell.* New York: Arno Press, 1974.

A Citizen of Lowell. *Corporations and Operatives: Being an Exposition of the Condition [of the] Factory Operatives.* 1843. Reprinted in *Women of Lowell.* New York: Arno Press, 1974.

Clark, Christopher. "The Household Economy: Market Exchange and the Rise of Capitalism in the Connecticut Valley, 1800-1860." *Journal of Social History* 13 (Winter 1979): 169-89.

Dalzell, Robert F. *Enterprising Elite: The Boston Associates and the World They Made.* Cambridge, MA: Harvard University Press, 1987.

Dublin, Thomas. *Women at Work: The Transformation of Work and Community in Lowell, Massachusetts, 1826-1860.* New York: Columbia University Press, 1979.

Eisler, Benita, ed. *The "Lowell Offering": Writings by New England Mill Women, 1840-1845.* Philadelphia: Lippincott, 1977.

"Factory Rules from the Handbook to Lowell, 1848." http://www.kentlaw.edu/ilhs/lowell.htm

Hood, Adrienne D. "The Gender Division of Labor in the Production of Textiles in Eighteenth-Century Rural Pennsylvania." *Journal of Social History* 27 (Spring 1994). http://www.searchbank.com/infotrac/session/4/0/82904/37xrn_7.

Kulikoff, Allan. "The Transition to Capitalism in Rural America." *William and Mary Quarterly* 46 (1989): 120-44.

Larcom, Lucy. "Among Lowell Mill Girls: A Reminiscence." 1881. Reprinted in *Women of Lowell.* New York: Arno Press, 1974.

Mohanty, Gail Fowler. "Handloom Outwork and Outwork Weaving in Rural Rhode Island, 1810-1821." *American Studies* 30 (Fall 1989): 41-68.

Prude, Jonathan. *The Coming of Industrial Order: Town and Factory Life in Rural Massachusetts, 1810-1860.* Cambridge: Cambridge University Press, 1983.

Robinson, Harriet H. *Loom and Spindle; Or, Life among the Early Mill Girls.* 1898. Reprinted in *Women of Lowell.* New York: Arno Press, 1974.

Sins of Our Mothers. Videocassette. Boston: PBS Video, 1988.

D5-g Models of professional writing in history

RESEARCH PAPERS

Cohen, Lizabeth. "From Town Center to Shopping Center: The Reconfiguration of Community Marketplaces in Postwar America." *American Historical Review* 101, no. 4 (1996): 1050-81.

Kishlansky, Mark. "Tyranny Denied: Charles I, Attorney General Heath, and the Five Knights' Case." *Historical Journal* 42, no. 1 (1999): 53-83.

BOOK REVIEW

Greenberg, David. Review of *Richard Nixon and the Quest for a New Majority,* by Robert Mason. *Journal of American History* 92, no. 3 (2005): 1068-69.

D6

Writing in nursing

Writing is an important tool in the education of nursing students as well as in the everyday workplaces of the profession. For students learning to become nurses, writing about specific nursing theories and practices, medical cases, and client experiences helps them better understand concepts and skills through research and analytical thinking.

For professional nurses, writing is a crucial mode of communication with colleagues in the health care profession, communication that can improve the quality of care for patients, or "clients," as they are increasingly called. Nurses write charts about their clients (a practice called *charting*), staff memos, patient education booklets, and policies for using a health care facility. They may also contribute research articles to journals in the field or craft arguments to persuade decision makers to change or adopt a particular health care policy.

To write effectively in nursing, you need to support claims with accurate client observations and current, researched evidence.

D6-a Recognize the forms of writing in nursing.

Students in nursing school are asked to write many different kinds of papers. You might encounter some of the following types of assignments:

- statements of philosophy
- nursing practice papers
- case studies
- research papers
- literature reviews
- experiential or reflective narratives
- position papers

Statements of philosophy

To help you articulate why you wish to become a nurse, your instructor may ask you to write your personal philosophy of nursing at the beginning of your professional schooling. This assignment is an opportunity to explain what principles you value, what experiences have shaped your career path, how you plan to put your principles into practice, and perhaps what specialization you are interested in pursuing.

Nursing practice papers

Assignments that ask you to apply your growing knowledge about medicine and care practices can take different forms: a nursing care plan, a concept map, or a nursing process paper. For these practice papers, you offer your readers

- a detailed client history and a nursing diagnosis of the client's health problems
- the interventions you recommend for the client
- your rationales for the interventions
- expected outcomes for your client
- actual, observed outcomes

A concept map is both an assignment type and an important technique that students can use to understand how to approach a question that arises in nursing care, such as how to care for a client with a particular illness. Students create a visual diagram that shows the connections between the possible diagnoses, the client and medical research data that could support each diagnosis, and the plans for client care that follow from each diagnosis.

Case studies

When you are asked to do a case study, you are given detailed information about a sample client's health issue and instructed to analyze the data. Case studies help you develop a global view of the many elements that make up a client's health problems and shape the health care decisions you make for your client. In a case study, you might

- interpret laboratory results
- evaluate data from a chart that a nurse on the previous shift has completed
- prioritize the client's medical needs
- determine the necessary guidelines for carrying out any required procedures (such as wound care)
- consider—with sensitivity—how the client's personal history, including language and cultural background, might inform how you interact with the client, answer questions, and respond to his or her needs

Research papers

A research paper assignment calls on you to research and report on a topic relevant to the nursing field—perhaps a particular disease, such as Alzheimer's, or an issue that challenges medical professionals, such as maintaining quality care when the downsizing of nursing staffs leads to longer, more fatiguing shifts. Typically, you are required to use as sources as many as twenty-five scholarly articles published in peer-reviewed journals in medical fields. (Peer-reviewed journals publish manuscripts only after they have been carefully reviewed anonymously by experts in the field.)

In some cases, you will be asked to formulate a research question (such as "Is the use of animal-assisted therapy effective in managing behavioral problems of Alzheimer's patients?") and come to a conclusion based on a review of recently published research. In other cases, you may be expected to synthesize information from a number of published articles to answer various questions about a nursing practice, such as medication administration, or about a disorder, such as muscular dystrophy.

Literature reviews

Review assignments ask you to read and synthesize published work on a nursing topic. Since as a nursing student you must read many scholarly articles about medical conditions and nursing practices, it is important to understand and stay current with the latest advances in the field. In a literature review, you summarize the arguments or findings of one or more journal articles or a larger body of recent scholarship on a topic. In some cases, you may be asked more specifically to analyze the works critically, evaluating whether the findings seem justified by the data. Such an assignment may be called a *critical review*.

Experiential or reflective narratives

Some of the writing you do as a nursing student will be reflective. To begin to understand what clients are experiencing because of an illness, you might write a personal narrative about what happened to you while caring for a client or what happened to your client as he or she coped with an illness. For example, one student wrote about the increasing sense of isolation and hopelessness that an elderly woman suffered because of her late-stage glaucoma.

Position papers

In a position paper, you take a stance on a controversial issue in the field, such as whether the government should prohibit junk food commercials during children's television programming. You must support your argument with evidence from published research and show the evidence and reasoning that may support an opposing position. A good position paper makes clear why the issue is controversial and important to debate.

D6-b Know the questions nurses ask.

Nursing students ask questions in their writing that ultimately help them effectively care for clients. Their questions, such as the following, involve understanding the needs of their clients:

- What information should you collect each day from a client with a particular condition?
- Do the client's data in the chart indicate a normal or an abnormal status of his or her condition?
- What interventions should you take based on the diagnosis of the client's condition? Why are those interventions necessary?
- How do you care for a surgical patient with chronic pain?

D6-c Understand the kinds of evidence nurses use.

When you are writing a paper in nursing, sometimes your evidence will be quantitative (such as lab results or a client's vital signs), and sometimes it will be qualitative (such as your observations and descriptions of a client's appearance or state of mind). The following are examples of the kinds of evidence you might use:

- a client's lab test results
- data from a nurse's client chart
- the research findings in a journal article
- direct observation of a client's physical or mental state

Because clients can have multiple medical problems that need to be prioritized for treatment, nurses use evidence to support more than one nursing diagnosis.

D6-d Become familiar with writing conventions in nursing.

Nurses agree on several conventions when they write:

- Nurses increasingly refer to the people in their care as "clients," not "patients."
- Evaluations and conclusions must be based on accurate and detailed information ("At the time of his diagnosis, the client had experienced a 20-lb weight loss in the previous 6 months. His CBC showed a WBC count of 32, an H & H of 13/38, and a platelet count of 34,000").
- *I* is acceptable in reflective papers about your own experience, but an objective voice is used for research papers, reviews, case studies, position papers, and papers detailing nursing practices ("Postoperative findings: External fixation devices extend from the proximal tibia and fibular shafts of the left foot").
- Nurses often use passive voice in describing procedures or recording their observations ("Inflammation was observed at the site of the incision").
- The identity of clients whose cases are discussed in writing must remain confidential (nurses often make up initials to denote a client's name).
- Direct quotation of sources is rare; instead, nurses paraphrase to demonstrate their understanding of the source material and to convey information economically.
- The APA (American Psychological Association) system of headings and subheadings helps readers see the hierarchy of sections in a paper.

D6-e   Use the APA system in writing in nursing.

Writers in nursing typically use the style guidelines of the American Psychological Association (APA) for formatting their paper, for citing sources in the text of their paper, and for listing sources at the end. The APA system is set forth in the *Publication Manual of the American Psychological Association*, 5th ed. (Washington: APA, 2001). (For more details, see APA-4 and APA-5 in *A Writer's Reference*, Sixth Edition.)

D6-f   Sample student paper: Nursing practice paper

If you are asked to write a nursing practice paper, you will need to provide a detailed client history, a nursing diagnosis of the client's health problem, the interventions you recommend to care for the client and your rationales, and the expected and actual outcomes for your client. The following student paper was written for a nursing course that focused on clinical experience. The writer, Julie Riss, used the style guidelines of the American Psychological Association (APA) to format her paper and to cite and list her sources.

ALL and HTN in One Client   i

Short title and page number in header on student papers. Lowercase roman numerals are used on the title page, arabic numerals on text pages.

If you are submitting a paper to a journal for publication, on the title page you will add the title or a shortened title below the header in all capital letters to be used as a running head in the journal.

Acute Lymphoblastic Leukemia and Hypertension in One Client:

A Nursing Practice Paper

Title page consists of a descriptive title in the center of the page and the writer's name, the course, the instructor, and the date centered at the bottom of the page.

Julie Riss

Nursing 451

Professor Durham

May 18, 2006

Marginal annotations indicate APA-style formatting and effective writing.

D6-f

Writing in nursing

Headings and subheadings, in APA style, mark the sections of the report and help readers follow the organization.

Riss begins by summarizing the client's history using information from his chart and her interview.

Riss respects the client's privacy by using only his initials in her paper.

Riss describes her detailed assessment of the client, using appropriate medical terminology.

Historical and Physical Assessment

Physical History

E.B. is a 16-year-old white male 179 cm tall weighing 86.9 kg. He was admitted to the hospital on April 14, 2006, due to decreased platelets and a need for a PRBC transfusion. He was diagnosed in October 2005 with T-cell acute lymphoblastic leukemia (ALL), after a 2-week period of decreased energy, decreased oral intake, easy bruising, and petechia. The client had experienced a 20-lb weight loss in the previous 6 months. At the time of diagnosis, his CBC showed a WBC count of 32, an H & H of 13/38, and a platelet count of 34,000. His initial chest X-ray showed an anterior mediastinal mass. Echocardiogram showed a structurally normal heart. He began induction chemotherapy on October 12, 2005, receiving vincristine, 6-mercaptopurine, doxorubicin, intrathecal methotrexate, and then high-dose methotrexate per protocol. During his hospital stay he required packed red cells and platelets on two different occasions. He was diagnosed with hypertension (HTN) due to systolic blood pressure readings consistently ranging between 130s and 150s and was started on nifedipine. E.B. has a history of mild ADHD, migraines, and deep vein thrombosis (DVT). He has tolerated the induction and consolidation phases of chemotherapy well and is now in the maintenance phase, in which he receives a daily dose of mercaptopurine, weekly doses of methotrexate, and intermittent doses of steroids.

Psychosocial History

There is a possibility of a depressive episode a year previously when he would not attend school. He got into serious trouble and was sent to a shelter for 1 month. He currently lives with his mother, father, and 14-year-old sister.

Family History

Paternal: prostate cancer and hypertension in grandfather

Maternal: breast cancer and heart disease

Current Assessment

Client's physical exam reveals him to be alert and oriented to person, place, and time. He communicates, though not readily. His speech and vision are intact. He has an equal grip bilaterally and can move all extremities, though he is generally weak. Capillary refill is less than 2 s. His peripheral pulses are strong and equal, and he is positive for posterior tibial and dorsalis pedis bilaterally. His lungs are clear to auscultation, his respiratory rate is 16, and his oxygen saturation is 99% on room air. He has positive bowel sounds in all quadrants, and his abdomen is soft, round, and nontender. He is on a regular diet, but his appetite has been poor. Client is voiding appropriately and his urine is clear and yellow. He appears pale and is unkempt. His skin is warm, dry, and intact. He has alopecia as a result of chemotherapy. His mediport site has no redness or inflammation. He appears somber and is slow to comply with nursing instructions.

Medical Diagnosis #1: Acute Lymphoblastic Leukemia

Leukemia is a neoplastic disease that involves the blood-forming tissues of the bone marrow, spleen, and lymph nodes. In leukemia the ratio of red to white blood cells is reversed. There are approximately 2,500 cases of acute lymphoblastic leukemia (ALL) per year in the United States, and it is the most common type of leukemia in children--it accounts for 75%-80% of childhood leukemias. The peak age of onset is 4 years, and it affects whites more often than blacks and males more often than females. Risk factors include Down syndrome or genetic disorders; exposures to ionizing radiation and certain chemicals such as benzene; human T-cell leukemia/lymphoma virus-1; and treatment for certain cancers. ALL causes an abnormal proliferation of lymphoblasts in the bone marrow, lymph nodes, and spleen. As the lymphoblasts proliferate, they suppress the other hematopoietic elements in the marrow. The leukemic cells do not function as mature cells and so do not work as they should in the immune and inflammatory processes. Because the growth of red blood cells and platelets is suppressed, the signs and symptoms of the disease are infections, bleeding, pallor, bone pain, weight loss, sore throat, fatigue, night sweats, and weakness. Treatment involves chemotherapy, bone marrow transplant, or stem cell transplant (Lemone & Burke, 2004).

Assessment uses a neutral tone.

APA allows extra space above headings when it improves readability.

Riss paraphrases the source and uses an APA-style in-text citation.

D6-f Writing in nursing

Medical Diagnosis #2: Hypertension

Primary hypertension in adolescence is a condition in which the blood pressure is persistently elevated to the 95th to 99th percentile for age, sex, and weight (Hockenberry, 2003). It must be elevated on three separate occasions for diagnosis to be made. Approximately 50 million people in the United States suffer from hypertension. It most often affects middle-aged and older adults and is more prevalent in black adults than in whites and Hispanics. In blacks the prevalence between males and females is equal, but in whites and Hispanics more males than females are affected. Risk factors include family history, age, race, mineral intake, obesity, insulin resistance, excess alcohol consumption, smoking, and stress. Hypertension results from sustained increases in blood volume and peripheral resistance. The increased blood volume causes an increase in cardiac output, which causes systemic arteries to vasoconstrict. This increased vascular resistance causes hypertension. Hypertension accelerates the rate of atherosclerosis, increasing the risk factor for heart disease and stroke. The workload of the heart is increased, causing ventricular hypertrophy, which increases risk for heart disease, dysrhythmias, and heart failure. Early hypertension usually exhibits no symptoms. The elevations in blood pressure are temporary at first but then progress to being permanent. A headache in the back of the head when awakening may be the only symptom. Other symptoms include blurred vision, nausea and vomiting, and nocturia. Treatment involves medications such as ACE inhibitors, diuretics, beta adrenergic blockers, calcium channel blockers, and vasodilators as well as changes in diet, such as decreased sodium intake. An increase in physical activity is essential to aid in weight loss and to reduce stress (Lemone & Burke, 2004).

Chart Review

Active Orders:

Vital signs q4h

Fall precautions

OOB as tolerated

Riss demonstrates her understanding of the medical condition.

ALL and HTN in One Client   4

Oximetry monitoring--continuous

CBC with manual differential daily in am

Regular diet

Weight--daily

Strict intake and output monitoring

Type and cross match

PRBCs--2 units

Platelets--1 unit

Discharge after CBC results posttransfusion shown to MD

Rationale for Orders

Vital signs are monitored every four hours per unit standard. In addition, the client's hypertension is an indication for close monitoring of blood pressure. He has generalized weakness, so fall precautions should be implemented. Though he is weak, ambulation is important, especially considering the client's history of DVT. A regular diet is ordered--I'm not sure why the client is not on a low-sodium diet, given his hypertension. Intake and output monitoring is standard on the unit. His hematological status needs to be carefully monitored due to his anemia and thrombocytopenia; therefore he has a CBC with manual differential done each morning. In addition, his hematological status is checked posttransfusion to see if the blood and platelets he receives increase his RBC and platelet counts. Transfused platelets survive in the body approximately 1-3 days, and the peak effect is achieved about 2 hr posttransfusion. Though platelets normally do not have to be cross-matched for blood group or type, children who receive multiple transfusions may become sensitized to a platelet group other than their own. Therefore, platelets are cross-matched with the donor's blood components. Blood and platelet transfusions may result in hemolytic, febrile, or allergic reactions, so the client is carefully monitored during the transfusion. Hospital protocol requires a set of baseline vital signs prior to transfusion vital signs. After the blood and platelets have been given, the physician is apprised of CBC results to be sure that the client's thrombocytopenia has resolved before he is discharged.

Riss uses specialized medical terminology.

Riss shows how physiology, prescribed treatments, and nursing practices are related.

ALL and HTN in One Client   5

Pharmacological Interventions and Goals

Short tables, like this one, are placed within the text. A longer table can be placed on a separate page.

Medications and Effects

ondansetron hydrochloride (Zofran) 8 mg PO PRN	serotonin receptor antagonist, antiemetic--prevention of nausea and vomiting associated with chemotherapy
famotidine (Pepcid) 10 mg PO ac	H2 receptor antagonist, antiulcer agent--prevention of heartburn
nifedipine (Procardia) 30 mg PO bid	calcium channel blocker, antihypertensive--prevention of hypertension
enoxaparin sodium (Lovenox) 60 mg SQ bid	low-molecular-weight heparin derivative, anticoagulant--prevention of DVT
mercaptopurine (Purinethol) 100 mg PO qhs	antimetabolite, antineoplastic-- treatment of ALL
PRBCs--2 units leukoreduced, irradiated[a]	to increase RBC count
platelets--1 unit[a]	to treat thrombocytopenia

[a]Because these products are dispensed by pharmacy, they are considered a pharmacological intervention, even though technically not medications.

Laboratory Tests and Significance

Riss presents data in several tables for easy reference.

Complete Blood Count (CBC)[a]

Result name	Result	Abnormal	Normal range
WBC	3.0	*	4.5-13.0
RBC	3.73	*	4.20-5.40
Hgb	11.5		11.1-15.7
Hct	32.4	*	34.0-46.0
MCV	86.8		78.0-95.0
MCH	30.7		26.0-32.0
MCHC	35.4		32.0-36.0
RDW	14.6		11.5-15.5
Platelet	98	*	140-400
MPV	8.3		7.4-10.4

[a]*Rationale:* Client's ALL diagnosis and treatment necessitate frequent monitoring of his hematological status. WBC count is decreased due to chemotherapy, as are RBC and hematocrit. The platelet count is low as well.

ALL and HTN in One Client   6

Type and Cross-Match[a]

Result name	Result
ABORH	APOS
ANTIBODY SCR INTERP	NEGATIVE

[a]*Rationale:* To determine client's blood type and to screen for antibodies.

Vital Signs before, during, and after Blood Transfusion[a]

Vital signs	Time	BP	Pulse	Resp	Temp (oral)
Pre	1705	113/74	92	18	98.7
15 min	1720	118/74	104	12	98.3
30 min	1735	121/74	96	16	99.3
45 min	1750	129/76	101	16	99.3
Post	1805	108/59	99	15	98.9

[a]*Rationale:* To monitor for reaction.

Nursing Diagnosis #1:

Injury, Risk for, Related to Decreased Platelet

Count and Administration of Lovenox

Desired Outcome: Client will remain free of injury.

Interventions:

Monitor vital signs q4h

Assess for manifestations of bleeding such as

- Skin and mucous membranes for petechiae, ecchymoses, and hematoma formation
- Gums and nasal membranes for bleeding
- Overt or occult blood in stool or urine
- Neurologic changes

Provide sponge to clean gums and teeth

Apply pressure to puncture sites for 3-5 min

Avoid invasive procedures when possible

Administer stool softeners as prescribed

Implement fall precautions

Monitor lab values for platelets

Administer platelets as prescribed

Measurable Outcomes:

Mediport site will remain intact with no signs of bleeding.

Riss prioritizes her diagnoses and recommended interventions and gives a detailed description and rationales for each.

Urine and stool will remain free of blood.

Lab values for anticoagulant therapy will remain in desired range.

Platelet count will remain in normal range.

Client Teaching:

Riss uses specific examples.

Instruct client to avoid forcefully blowing nose, straining to have a
bowel movement, and forceful coughing or sneezing, all of
which increase the risk for external and internal bleeding

Discharge Planning:

Instruct client to monitor for signs of decreased platelet count such
as easy bruising, petechiae, or inappropriate bleeding

Nursing Diagnosis #2:

Infection, Risk for, Related to Depressed Body Defenses

Desired Outcome: Client will remain free of infection.

Interventions:

Screen all visitors and staff for signs of infection to minimize
exposure to infectious agents

Use aseptic technique for all procedures

Monitor temperature to detect possible infection

Evaluate client for potential sites of infection: needle punctures,
mucosal ulcerations

Provide nutritionally complete meals to support the body's natural
defenses

Monitor lab values for CBC

Administer G-CSF if prescribed

Measurable Outcomes:

Mediport site will remain free of erythema, purulent drainage, odor,
and edema.

Client will remain afebrile.

Client Teaching:

Instruct client and caregivers in correct hand-washing technique

Discharge Planning:

Instruct client and caregivers to avoid live attenuated virus vaccines

Instruct client to avoid large crowds

Nursing Diagnosis #3:

Noncompliance, Related to HTN, as Evidenced by Lack of

Consistent Medication Regimen and Adherence to Dietary Plan

Desired Outcome: Client will follow treatment plan.

Interventions:

Inquire about reasons for noncompliance

Listen openly and without judgment

Evaluate knowledge of HTN, its long-term effects, and treatment

Arrange for nutritional consult with dietitian

Measurable Outcomes:

Client will take medication as prescribed.

Client's systolic blood pressure will remain in normal range.

Client Teaching:

Instruct on medication regimen: appropriate administration and

potential adverse effects

Provide information on hypertension and its treatment

Discharge Planning:

Provide prescriptions

Nursing Diagnosis #4:

Health Maintenance, Ineffective, Related to

Unhealthy Lifestyle and Behaviors

Desired Outcome: Client will make changes in lifestyle.

Interventions:

Assist in identifying behaviors that contribute to hypertension

Assist in developing a realistic health maintenance plan including

modifying risk factors such as exercise, diet, and stress

Help client and family identify strengths and weaknesses in

maintaining health

Measurable Outcomes:

Client will verbalize ways to control his hypertension.

Client will identify methods to relieve stress.

Discharge Planning:

Provide information on possible exercise programs

D6-f

Analysis

Riss summarizes the client's conditions, treatments, and consequences for nursing and discusses client education in psychological and social contexts.

In the case of E.B., there are two separate disease processes at work--ALL and HTN. The ALL is the most immediately pressing of the two and is indirectly responsible for the client's current hospitalization. The chemotherapy treatment for his leukemia has caused thrombocytopenia. This condition places him at high risk for hemorrhage. The anticoagulant therapy for DVT increases this risk even further, not only because it may cause bleeding complications, but because in itself it may cause thrombocytopenia. Therefore, it is imperative to raise his platelet count as quickly as possible. Surprisingly, there were no lab tests ordered to determine his PT and INR, both of which are monitored when a client is on anticoagulant therapy. As his CBC demonstrates, not only is his platelet count low, but his red blood cells are decreased. That is why his physician ordered a transfusion of both PRBCs and platelets.

In terms of E.B.'s diagnosis of HTN, he has a positive family history, which is a major risk factor for developing the disease. Excess weight is also a risk factor, and the client has a history of obesity as well. Because exercise is an important factor in managing the excess weight and stress associated with the disease, his leukemia and the chemotherapy treatments aimed at curing E.B.'s leukemia actually negatively affect his ability to manage the hypertension: He is often too weak and fatigued to participate in much physical activity. Additionally, the steroids have resulted in added weight gain, increasing instead of decreasing the problem. To date, the client has failed to maintain a favorable diet regimen.

E.B.'s family circumstances must be taken into consideration when managing his treatment. Though he resides with both parents, there is some question as to the support and consistency of care he receives. He often appears very unkempt and is at times noncompliant with his hypertension medication. Due to his parents' inability to care for a central venous line (CVL) at home, he has a mediport that can be accessed as needed but requires care. On a positive note, the father is aware of their limitations and tries to work with the staff to make sure that E.B.'s ALL is managed appropriately.

References

Hockenberry, M. (2003). *Wong's nursing care of infants and children.* St. Louis, MO: Mosby.

Lemone, P., & Burke, K. (2004). *Medical surgical nursing critical thinking in client care.* Upper Saddle River, NJ: Pearson Education.

Riss provides a reference list for sources she cited in her paper. The list is formatted in APA style.

D6-g Models of professional writing in nursing

NURSING PRACTICE PAPER

Miller, D., & MacDonald, D. (2006). Management of pediatric patients with chronic kidney disease. *Pediatric Nursing, 32*(2), 128-135.

RESEARCH PAPER

Coyer, S. M., Plonczynski, D. J., Baldwin, K. B., & Fox, P. G. (2006). Screening for violence against women in a rural health care clinic. *Online Journal of Rural Nursing and Health Care, 6*(1). Retrieved July 2, 2006, from http://www.rno.org/journal/issues/Vol-6/issue-1/Coyer_article.htm

LITERATURE REVIEWS

Ingersoll, S., Valente, S. M., & Roper, J. (2005). Nurse care coordination for diabetes. *Journal of Nursing Care Quality, 20*(3), 208-214.

Murphy, C. (2006). The 2003 SARS outbreak: Global challenges and innovative infection control measures. *Online Journal of Issues in Nursing, 11*(1). Retrieved July 2, 2006, from http://www.nursingworld.org/ojin/topic29/tpc29_5.htm

POSITION PAPER

Hospice and Palliative Nurses Association. (2003). HPNA position paper: Complementary therapies. *Journal of Hospice & Palliative Nursing, 5*(2), 113-117.

D7

Writing in psychology

Psychologists write for various audiences and with various purposes in mind. They frequently publish articles about their research for their colleagues, or they present their work at professional conferences. They write proposals to convince funding agencies to award grants for their research. If they teach, psychologists also write lectures. Sometimes psychologists write to influence the opinions held by the public or by decision makers in government, lending their expertise to discussions on such issues as the effects of racism, the challenges of aging, or children's mental health. For these readers, psychologists may write analyses for newspaper and magazine op-ed pages as well as policy recommendations and advocacy statements.

Writing in psychology relies on an approach found in the social sciences and sciences: Papers need to deliver information to readers efficiently, logically, and neutrally. When you write for psychology courses, your challenge will be to present data and analysis succinctly and accurately.

D7-a Recognize the forms of writing in psychology.

When you take courses in psychology, you may be asked to write any of the following:

- literature reviews
- research papers
- theoretical papers
- poster presentations

Literature reviews

You will likely write review papers early in your course work. In a review paper, you report on and evaluate the research that has been published in the field about a particular topic. A literature review does not merely summarize researchers' findings but argues a position with evidence that you assemble from the empirical (that is, experiment-based) studies that you review.

Sometimes a literature review stands alone as a paper, such as a survey of findings from research performed in the past century on the question of what causes loss of memory in old age. In some cases, you will be asked to write a critical review, in which you will analyze the methods and interpretations of data in one or more journal articles. More often a literature review is an introduction to a larger piece of writing, such as a report of your own empirical study. In that case, the literature review surveys previously published findings relevant to the question that the empirical study investigates.

Research papers

When instructors refer to "research papers," they may have different assignments in mind. A research paper might present your synthesis of many sources of information about, say, emotional responses to music. Your purpose would be to demonstrate your understanding of various research findings and the ongoing debates emerging from researchers' investigations.

A research paper might also be a report on the results of an experiment you've conducted and on your interpretation of those results; in this case, your research paper would be an empirical study. A research paper could also relate your interpretations to what others in the field have concluded from their own experiments. Like other scientists, psychologists publish research papers in journals after the papers have undergone rigorous and impartial review by other psychologists (called *peer review*) to make sure that the scientific process used by the researchers is sound.

Whether published in a journal or written for a college course, research papers based on original experiments have the following standard elements:

- the question you want to research and why your question is important
- a review of research relevant to your question
- your hypotheses (tentative, plausible answers to the research question that your experiment will test) and your predictions that follow from the hypotheses
- the method you used to conduct your experiment
- the results from the experiment
- your analysis of those results

Writers of research reports also use tables and figures to present experimental data in easy-to-grasp visual form.

Theoretical papers

Psychologists often write theoretical papers in which they propose their own theories or extend existing theories about a research problem in the field. For example, in one journal article, a psychologist argues that the field needs to combine attachment theory and social network theory to understand child and adolescent development.

If you are asked to write a theoretical paper for a course, you will be expected to support the theory you propose by pointing to evidence and counterevidence from the literature in the field, to compare your theory with others, and possibly to suggest experiments that could test your theory more rigorously.

Poster presentations

At professional gatherings such as annual conventions, psychologists have the opportunity to present their work in the form of a poster rather than as a formal talk. Conference attendees approach presenters in an exhibit area to talk about their research, which the posters concisely summarize. A poster features an introduction to the project, the method, information about the experiment's subjects, the results, and the presenter's conclusions.

Poster presentations also feature graphs and tables since it is important to convey information to the audience quickly and concisely as they walk through the exhibit area. An effective poster presentation will encourage the audience to ask questions and carry on an informal conversation with the presenter.

Your instructor may ask you to create a poster presentation about an experiment you or other researchers have conducted both to help you understand complex concepts and to practice your communication skills.

NOTE: Some presenters use presentation software to create a slide show that they can click through for a small audience or project on a screen for a larger group. Presenters generally include the same kinds of information in slide presentations as they do in poster presentations.

D7-b Know the questions psychologists ask.

Psychologists generally investigate human behavior and perceptions. Their questions range widely across the different specializations that make up the field, such as animal cognition, personality, social interactions, and infant development, to name a few. The following are questions that specialists in psychology might ask:

- What personality characteristics might affect employees' personal use of work computers?
- What is the impact on adult learners' families and working lives when they return to school?
- Do variations in cerebral blood flow in different areas of the brain predict variations in performance of different imagery tasks?

D7-c Understand the kinds of evidence psychologists use.

To back up their conclusions, psychologists look for evidence in case studies and the results of experiments. They do not use expert opinion as evidence; direct quotations of what other psychologists have written are rare in psychology papers. Instead, papers focus on data (the results of experiments) and on the analysis of the results that the writer has collected.

Depending on their specialization, psychologists may ask questions that lead to quantitative or qualitative research and data. Quantitative research and data involve numerical measurement of phenomena; qualitative research and data involve interviews of subjects and the researcher's verbal descriptions of observations.

- Quantitative evidence might be facts and statistics: "Regional cerebral blood flow in a total of 26 areas predicted performance, and 20 of these areas predicted performance only in a single task"; "In a study on what motivates adolescents to quit smoking, 44.7% of the participants reported that they wanted to quit because their parents wanted them to." Or it might be results of original experiments: "Fraudulent excuse scores were correlated with cheating scores ($r = .37, n = 211, p < .0001$)."

- Qualitative evidence is usually examples and illustrations: "Many of the respondents believed girls' tendency either to address indirectly or to avoid conflict was supported by adults, who expected them to be *ladylike*; when asked to define this term, they used such descriptors as 'mature' and 'calm.'"

D7-d Become familiar with writing conventions in psychology.

Psychologists use straightforward and concise language and depend on special terms to explain their findings.

- Specialized vocabulary may include terms such as *methods, results, double-blind study, social identity perspective,* and *nonverbal emotions.*

- Often researchers use specific, technical definitions of terms that nonspecialists use differently. For example, if a psychologist asks whether adults with eating disorders are "depressed," the term refers to a specific mental disorder, not to a general mood of sadness.

- When reporting conclusions, writers in psychology use the past tense (*Berkowitz found*) or the present perfect tense (*Berkowitz has found*). When discussing results, they use the present tense (*The results confirm*). They avoid using subjective phrases like *I think* and *I feel.*

D7-e Use the APA system in writing in psychology.

Writers in psychology typically use the style guidelines of the American Psychological Association (APA) for formatting their papers, for citing sources in the text of their papers, and for listing sources at the end. The APA system is set forth in the *Publication Manual of the American Psychological Association*, 5th ed. (Washington: APA, 2001). (For more details, see APA-4 and APA-5 in *A Writer's Reference*, Sixth Edition.)

D7-f Sample student paper: Literature review (excerpt)

A psychology literature review assignment usually asks you both to survey published research on a topic in the field and to argue your own position with evidence that you assemble from published studies. The student paper excerpted beginning on page D-80 was written for a second-year developmental psychology course. The student, Valerie Charat, used the style guidelines of the American Psychological Association (APA) to format her paper and to cite and list her sources.

Short title and page number in header on student papers. Lowercase roman numerals are used on preliminary pages such as the title page and abstract page, arabic numerals on text pages.

ADHD in Boys vs. Girls   i

Descriptive title, centered on the page.

Always Out of Their Seats (and Fighting):

Why Are Boys Diagnosed with ADHD More Often Than Girls?

Writer's name, course, instructor, and date, centered at the bottom of the page.

Valerie Charat

Psychology 1806

Professor Korfine

December 15, 2006

Marginal annotations indicate APA-style formatting **and** effective writing.

ADHD in Boys vs. Girls   ii

Abstract

Until the early 1990s, most research on attention deficit
hyperactivity disorder (ADHD) focused on boys and did not explore
possible gender differences. Recent studies have suggested that
gender differences do exist and are caused by personality differences
between boys and girls, by gender bias in referring teachers and
clinicians, or by the diagnostic procedures themselves. But the most
likely reason is that ADHD is often comorbid--that is, it coexists
with other behavior disorders that are not diagnosed properly and
that do exhibit gender differences. This paper first considers studies
of gender differences only in ADHD and then looks at studies of
gender differences when ADHD occurs with comorbid disorders.
Future research must focus more specifically on how gender
differences are influenced by factors such as referrals, family history,
and comorbid conditions.

Abstract, a 100-
to-120-word
overview of the
paper, appears
on a separate
page.

D7-f Writing in psychology

Full title, repeated on page 1.

Charat gives abbreviations in parentheses the first time she uses common psychology terms.

Introduction provides background to the topic and establishes why a literature review on ADHD is necessary.

Thesis states what Charat will argue by describing and analyzing the sources she has reviewed.

Charat uses APA style to cite her sources. Two sources in one parenthetical citation are separated by a semicolon.

Headings, centered, divide the paper into two main sections.

Always Out of Their Seats (and Fighting):
Why Are Boys Diagnosed with ADHD More Often Than Girls?

Attention deficit hyperactivity disorder (ADHD) is a commonly diagnosed disorder in children that affects social, academic, or occupational functioning. As the name suggests, its hallmark characteristics are hyperactivity and lack of attention as well as impulsive behavior. For decades, studies have focused on the causes, expression, prevalence, and outcome of the disorder, but until recently very little research investigated gender differences. In fact, until the early 1990s most research focused exclusively on boys (Brown, Madan-Swain, & Baldwin, 1991), perhaps because many more boys than girls are diagnosed with ADHD. Researchers have speculated on the possible explanations for the disparity, citing reasons such as true sex differences in the manifestation of the disorder's symptoms, gender biases in those who refer children to clinicians, and possibly even the diagnostic procedures themselves (Gaub & Carlson, 1997). But the most persuasive reason is that ADHD is often a comorbid condition--that is, it coexists with other behavior disorders that are not diagnosed properly and that do exhibit gender differences.

It has been suggested that in the United States children are often misdiagnosed as having ADHD when they actually suffer from a behavior disorder such as conduct disorder (CD) or a combination of ADHD and another behavior disorder (Disney, Elkins, McGue, & Iancono, 1999; Lilienfeld & Waldman, 1990). Conduct disorder is characterized by negative and criminal behavior in children and is highly correlated with adult diagnoses of antisocial personality disorder (ASPD). This paper first considers research that has dealt only with gender difference in the occurrence of ADHD and then looks at research that has studied the condition along with other behavior disorders.

Gender Differences in Studies of ADHD

Most of the research on ADHD has lacked a comparative component. Throughout the 1970s and 1980s, most research focused only on boys. If girls were included, it was often in such low

ADHD in Boys vs. Girls　2

numbers that gender-based comparisons were unwarranted (Gaub & Carlson, 1997). One of the least debated differences is the dissimilarity in male and female prevalence rates. Some studies have claimed a 3:1 ratio of boys with ADHD to girls with ADHD (American Psychiatric Association, 1987), while others have cited ratios as high as 9:1 (Brown et al., 1991). The differences in prevalence have been attributed to a variety of causes, one of which is that girls may have more internalized symptoms and may be overlooked in ADHD diagnoses (Brown et al., 1991).

　　　A study conducted by Breen (1989) sought to test the differences in cognition, behavior, and academic functioning for boys and girls. Past research had indicated that boys with ADHD showed more aggressive behavior while girls showed more learning problems, but the results were often conflicting. To clarify the existing information, Breen conducted a study on 39 children aged 6 to 11, from a group of children referred to a pediatric psychology clinic. All subjects were white, with varying socioeconomic status. He broke the subjects into three groups: boys with ADHD, girls with ADHD, and a control group of girls without any psychiatric or family history of behavioral or emotional problems. Each group was given a battery of tests to assess cognitive functioning. All children were also observed in a playroom while they worked math problems, and all were coded for a variety of behaviors including fidgeting, vocalizing, being out of their seats, and so on.

　　　The results showed that while both groups with ADHD performed nearly equally across most measures, ADHD boys were generally viewed as more deviant than normal girls. Girls with ADHD were closer behaviorally to girls in the control group than to ADHD boys. This finding indicates that it may be difficult to distinguish girls with ADHD from girls without the disorder based solely on behavior. This conclusion was corroborated by the later finding (Brown et al., 1991) that girls with ADHD are often not clinically referred unless they demonstrate a more severe form of the disorder than boys do. A contradictory finding (Breen, 1989) was that ADHD boys and girls displayed rates of disruptive behavior that were

Charat summarizes key research findings about the paper's central question.

A signal phrase names the author and gives the date of the source in parentheses.

Charat examines an important study in detail. She summarizes experimental methods used by researchers.

Charat uses the specialized language of the field.

not significantly different from each other, although Breen did not
indicate what forms the disruptive behavior took and whether the
girls were less aggressive than the boys. But as Brown et al. (1991)
later pointed out, it was easier to differentiate ADHD in externalized
behaviors--aggression, inattention, and overactivity--than in
internalized behaviors--depression, anxiety, and withdrawal. It is
striking, however, that the distinction in Breen's study was clearer
not between boys and girls but between girls with and girls without
ADHD. Breen concluded that differences between boys and girls with
the disorder do not seem significant.

A few drawbacks to Breen's study include a lack of screening
for comorbid conduct disorders, which were no doubt present in some
of the subjects. The small sample size could have hindered the
results, with only 13 subjects in each group. Another limitation is
the small cross-section: All subjects were white and clinically
referred. Therefore, the findings cannot be generalized to a
nonclinical, racially diverse population. Finally, the lack of male
controls is surprising, given the usual trend to overrepresent boys
when studying ADHD. A reasonable comparison would have been
between girls with ADHD and boys in a control group to see if the
girls' range of antisocial behavior was beyond that of control boys.

Another study (Maughan, Pickles, Hagell, Rutter, & Yule, 1996)
investigated the association between reading problems and
antisocial behavior. The researchers cited a connection that had
previously been made (Hinshaw, 1992, as cited in Maughan et al.,
1996) between antisocial behavior and underachievement in early
childhood, while aggression and antisocial behavior became salient
in later years. Maughan et al. looked specifically at reading because
research has shown that children who develop reading problems have
higher rates of behavioral problems even before they learn to read
(Jorm, Share, Matthews, & McLean, 1986). It had also been shown
that reading problems can affect behavioral development (Pianta &
Caldwell, 1992, as cited in Maughan et al., 1996). However, since
most studies had been done with boys, the researchers also
compared gender differences.

Source first
mentioned on
page 1. In
subsequent
citations, "et al."
is used after the
first author's
name in the
text and in
parentheses.

Charat analyzes
the study's
shortcomings.

Topic sentence
states para-
graph's main
point.

An indirect
source (work
quoted in an-
other source) is
indicated with
the words "as
cited in."

An ampersand
separates the
authors' names
in parentheses.

ADHD in Boys vs. Girls   4

Subjects were selected from a previously conducted study in a population of children who were 10 years old in 1970. The majority were British-born Caucasians of low socioeconomic status. The analysis used two subsamples, one with poor reading scores, the other a randomly sampled control group with average IQ and no reading difficulties. Poor readers were rated as either "backward" or "retarded." The subjects in the backward group were 28 months below average in reading level for their age and IQ. At age 10, children had received psychometric testing, and the study accounted for parental occupation, the child's government benefits status, and the ranking of the child's state school in terms of economic adversity. There were follow-ups at ages 14, 17, and early 20s.

Poor readers demonstrated high rates of behavior problems by age 10. About 40% of the girls and almost 50% of the boys in the retarded reading group exhibited antisocial behavior at age 10. Interestingly, reading-retarded girls showed high rates of conduct problems, while the boys did not. Also, among girls there were much higher rates of antisocial behavior in the lowest socioeconomic category than in slightly higher socioeconomic categories. In boys, the differences were not as pronounced. For boys, poor performance in school was the only predictor of antisocial behavior, while for girls poor school performance and reading level were predictors. This finding suggests that for boys, learning difficulties do not increase the risk of behavior problems, while for girls they do. Inattentiveness and overactivity were also related to reading problems and were highly related to antisocial behavior. When inattentiveness and overactivity were factored in, there were no direct links between reading difficulties and antisocial behavior. This absent connection means that reading problems do not cause antisocial behavior. It is when they cannot pay attention or sit long enough to read that both boys and girls exhibit elevated rates of antisocial behavior.

By age 14, girls still showed a significant correlation between reading problems and antisocial behavior while boys showed no association. In early adulthood (ages 17 and early 20s), criminality,

Charat describes the study's methods in detail.

In APA style, the numbers 10 and above are expressed in numerals; percentages are expressed in numbers with a percent symbol.

alcohol problems, aggression, and personality disorders were found in low rates in girls. In the sample of girls interviewed in their 20s, 1.9% had juvenile offense records and 5.4% had records of adult crime. In boys, poor readers did not show any significant rates of antisocial personality disorders.

The study had several drawbacks. Subject responses at follow-up periods were not uniformly gathered, and the lack of analysis of female juvenile offenders made it harder to understand

[Charat continues to describe and analyze researchers' studies and findings.]

Conclusion pre-
sents a synthe-
sis of the
paper's points.

Charat raises
questions about
the research she
reviews but
adopts a
balanced tone
in summarizing
the sources.

Charat suggests
areas for future
research.

Conclusion

Although the studies presented here are filled with flaws and contradictory findings, they have a unifying thread. Through direct findings or indirect lack of information, all suggest that the higher rate of male diagnoses of ADHD is not necessarily because the disorder actually occurs in boys more often than in girls. Although boys are more commonly diagnosed, this phenomenon could reflect a long-standing history of misperceptions. Since hyperactive and inattentive boys are also often aggressive and disruptive, girls who do not demonstrate similar behaviors may be overlooked.

It is important to reevaluate the way boys and girls are observed and understood when attention and hyperactivity are being assessed. Males and females may display different behaviors, and parents and teachers may interpret their behaviors differently. But when rated by trained researchers, boys and girls identified as having ADHD are rated similarly. However, it is easier to identify externalizing, aggressive behavior than it is to identify internalizing behavior, and this difference may be one of the main factors at the root of the perceived gender differences in the prevalence of ADHD. There is not enough concrete evidence to rule out the possibility that a gender difference does exist, regardless of the fact that boys and girls seem to show equal rates and degrees of symptoms. Until more studies look at population samples, exclude conduct disorders,

ADHD in Boys vs. Girls   11

and take into account possible differences in the ways the symptoms are manifested, it is impossible to conclude that gender differences are the result of social and clinical biases and stereotypes. Further research on genetics and familial rates of the disorder are also necessary to help clarify the relationship between adult antisocial personality disorder and ADHD. Also, until a clear distinction is made between conduct disorder and ADHD, not only in the text of the *DSM-IV* but also in the minds of laypeople and clinicians, it will be difficult to separate children with comorbid disorder and those without it and to assess gender differences as well.

Conclusion affirms the necessity of continuing investigation.

References

American Psychiatric Association. (1987). *Diagnostic and statistical manual of mental disorders* (3rd ed., rev.). Washington, DC: Author.

American Psychiatric Association. (1994). *Diagnostic and statistical manual of mental disorders* (4th ed.). Washington, DC: Author.

Breen, M. J. (1989). Cognitive and behavioral differences in ADHD boys and girls. *Journal of Child Psychology and Psychiatry, 30,* 711-716.

Breen, M. J., & Altepeter, T. S. (1990). Situational variability in boys and girls identified as ADHD. *Journal of Clinical Psychology, 46,* 486-490.

Brown, R. T., Madan-Swain, A., & Baldwin, K. (1991). Gender differences in a clinic-referred sample of attention-deficit-disordered children. *Child Psychiatry and Human Development, 22,* 111-127.

Disney, E. R., Elkins, J. J., McGue, M., & Iancono, W. G. (1999). Effects of ADHD, conduct disorder, and gender on substance use and abuse in adolescence. *American Journal of Psychiatry, 156,* 1515-1521.

Faraone, S. V., Biederman, J., Chen, W. J., Milberger, S., Warburton, R., & Tsuang, M. T. (1995). Genetic heterogeneity in attention-deficit hyperactivity disorder (ADHD): Gender, psychiatric comorbidity, and maternal ADHD. *Journal of Abnormal Psychology, 104,* 334-345.

Gaub, M., & Carlson, C. L. (1997). Gender differences in ADHD: A meta-analysis and critical review. *Journal of the American Academy of Child and Adolescent Psychiatry, 36,* 1036-1045. Retrieved November 29, 2006, from Expanded Academic ASAP database (A20143685).

Jorm, A. F., Share, D. L., Matthews, R., & McLean, R. (1986). Behaviour problems in specific reading retarded and general reading backward children: A longitudinal study. *Journal of Child Psychology and Psychiatry, 27,* 33-43.

Margin notes:

List of references begins on a new page. Heading is centered.

List is alphabetized by authors' last names. All authors' names are inverted; an ampersand separates the last two authors.

The first line of an entry is at the left margin; subsequent lines indented ½" (or five spaces).

A work with up to six authors lists all authors' names. A work with more than six authors lists the first six followed by "et al." (for "and others").

Double-spacing is used throughout.

D7-g   Models of professional writing in psychology

LITERATURE REVIEW

Wixted, J. T. (2004). The psychology and neuroscience of forgetting. *Annual Review of Psychology, 55*, 235-269.

RESEARCH PAPERS (EMPIRICAL STUDIES)

Crothers, L. M., Field, J. E., & Kolbert, J. B. (2005). Navigating power, control, and being nice: Aggression in adolescent girls' friendships. *Journal of Counseling and Development, 83*, 349-354.

Kosslyn, S. M., Thompson, W. L., & Shephard, J. M. (2004). Brain rCBF and performance in visual imagery tasks: Common and distinct processes. *European Journal of Cognitive Psychology, 16*, 696-716.

THEORETICAL PAPER

Levitt, M. J. (2005). Social relations in childhood and adolescence: The Convoy Model perspective. *Human Development, 48*, 28-47.

Index